PASSION FOR CREATION

MEISTER ECKHART'S CREATION SPIRITUALITY

INTRODUCTION AND
COMMENTARIES BY

MATTHEW FOX

SELECTIONS FROM *Breakthrough*

IMAGE
DOUBLEDAY
NEW YORK LONDON TORONTO SYDNEY AUCKLAND

BV
5080
.E3213
1995

For Ben, and others like him,
who have quietly and deeply
out of their own courage and integrity,
been living Eckhart's path unknowingly for years.

AN IMAGE BOOK
PUBLISHED BY DOUBLEDAY
a division of
Bantam Doubleday Dell Publishing Group, Inc.
1540 Broadway, New York, New York 10036

IMAGE, DOUBLEDAY, and the portrayal of a deer drinking
from a stream are trademarks of Doubleday,
a division of Bantam Doubleday Dell Publishing Group, Inc.

Sections have appeared in *Breakthrough: Meister Eckhart's
Creation Spirituality in New Translation*
Translation, Commentary Copyright © 1980 by Matthew Fox
Revisions, Introductions Copyright © 1995 by Matthew Fox
This Image Edition published November 1995.

Library of Congress Cataloging-in-Publication Data
Eckhart, Meister, d. 1327.
[Selections. English. 1995]
Passion for creation : Meister Eckhart's creation spirituality :
selections from Breakthrough / introduction and commentaries
by Matthew Fox.
p.   cm.
1. Mysticism—Early works to 1800.   2. Sermons, German—
Middle High German—Translations into English.   3. Sermons,
Latin—Translations into English.   I. Fox, Matthew, 1940–
II. Title.
BV5080.E3213 1995
248—dc20   95-37818
                                                           CIP

ISBN 0-385-48047-4
Copyright © 1995 by Doubleday, a division
of Bantam Doubleday Dell Publishing Group, Inc.
All Rights Reserved
Printed in the United States of America
1   3   5   7   9   10   8   6   4   2

Contents

INTRODUCTION

How Eckhart Lures Us
into the
Sacred Wilderness

Of all the mystics of the West, it is difficult to find anyone who more profoundly articulates the journey we make into the divine and out into the world again than Meister Eckhart. His is a spirituality of passion and compassion. Eckhart, a Dominican friar and preacher, lived from 1260 to 1329. Though some of his ideas were condemned by Pope John XXII a week after he died, scholars today agree that his condemnation was a political one and that enemies misconstrued his teachings. Eckhart made enemies because his mysticism was not one of flight from the world or of escape from engagement in the world. Rather, he teaches that spiritual awakening is to lead to justice-making and compassion in the world. He practiced what he preached, and since he was preaching justice and compassion as a deep spirituality, he was certain to step on the toes of the powerful and the arrogant. Two examples of this are his support of the Beguine movement which was the women's movement of the fourteenth century. And another is his support of the peasants. Indeed, half his sermons were preached in the peasant dialect of his day, and at his trial he was accused of "confusing the simple people" by telling them that they were all "aristocrats," or, "royal persons."

But this is precisely the heart of Eckhart's teaching and the heart of the biblical tradition of creation spirituality: That humans are blessed with divine powers and beauty but also with responsibilities of justice-making and compassion that characterize all royal personhood. How do we get to such deep self-esteem and to such deep acceptance of our responsibility? For, as Eckhart puts it, it is no good to be a king but not know one is a king. Our awareness is everything; our waking up is everything. We need to move from the superficial or "outer self" to the true self or "inner self." Who is this inner self? Eckhart answers this question in his treatise "On the Aristocrat," or, "On the Royal Person."

The inner person is the soil in which God has sown the divine likeness and image and in which God sows the good seed, the roots of all wisdom, all skills, all virtues, all goodness—the seed of the divine nature (2 Pt 1:4). . . . This is the good tree of which our Lord says that it always bears good fruit and never evil fruit. For it desires goodness and is inclined toward goodness. . . .

The seed of God is in us. If the seed had a good, wise, and industrious cultivator, it would thrive all the more and grow up to God whose seed it is, and the fruit would be equal to the nature of God. Now the seed of a pear tree grows into a pear tree, a hazel seed into a hazel tree, the seed of God into God (Cf. Jn 3:9). . . . Origen, one of the great masters of the spiritual life, says, however, that the Godself has sown this seed, and inserted it and borne it. Thus while this seed may be crowded, hidden away, and never cultivated, it will still never be obliterated. It glows and shines, gives off light, burns, and is unceasingly inclined toward God.

It is our task to cultivate this seed and give it nourishment so that the divine image in us can grow and thrive and prosper. This is what the spiritual journey is about. Our spiritual journey consists in nourishing and watering and caring for this God-seed that is in all of us.

Eckhart concludes the same treatise with a beautiful passage about our responsibility to be prophets and to soar like great birds. He talks of our need to recover the experience of the sacred wilderness, just as the prophet Hosea promised when he proposed that God wants to call us into the wilderness and there speak to us heart to heart. Eckhart writes:

> What our Lord calls a royal person is named by the prophet a large eagle. Who then is more royal than one who was born, on the one hand, from the highest and best that a creature possesses and, on the other hand, from the most intimate depths of the divine nature and its wilderness? Through the prophet Hosea our Lord says: "I am going to lure her and lead her out into the wilderness and speak to her heart" (Ho. 1:16). One with one, one from one, one in one, and eternally one in one. Amen.

We are all supremely royal because we have been born "from the highest and best that a creature possesses" *and* because we have been born "from the most intimate depths of the divine nature and its wilderness." Our humanity *and* our divinity compel us to be lured into the wilderness, enticed there, to grow our souls large and magnanimous. We are not to settle for just "eating our bread and drinking our beer" but to soar into the great wilderness that in fact is part of the divine nature.

The spiritual life is like that. It is not about tidiness but more about chaos; it is not about being boxed in but more about soaring beyond our boxes; it is not about being bored or suffering boredom, but more about being wild and entering wilderness. It is about passion, a holy passion.

The tasks at hand in our day—the ecological devastation, the despair of the young, the sterility of so many of our institutions from education to politics to economics to religion to art—all these require a leap into the sacred wilderness, an opening of the heart and mind and spirit to great things, to divine things, to our own royal personhood with all the dignity *and* all the responsibility implied in that holy lineage. Eckhart teaches that no matter what our wounds or the abuse we may have suffered and from whom, *none of us need remain in a victim state*. Rather, we are, each and every one of us, born of greatness and divine dignity. Our spiritual journey is a journey of finding that original goodness and blessing and beauty (the Via Positiva and the Via Negativa); and of living it out in society so that others

can find it (the Via Creativa and the Via Transformativa).

How does the journey begin? The late physicist
David Bohm said that he was developing a physics
"that begins with the whole." The Greek word for
"whole" is *kosmos*. Thus, a cosmology is the way to
begin our spiritual journey, a relating to the
whole. In this relationship awe and wonder come
alive, our energies and hopes and aspirations
catch fire. We move from the anthropocentrism
of the modern age that renders us passive and flat
and boring to the spirit that comes alive in a
"postmodern" age when cosmology comes alive
again. Here lies a spirituality for an ecological
time and an Environmental Revolution.

Eckhart is deeply cosmological. "All things
love God," Eckhart teaches, and nature itself
does the same. "For whether you wish it or not,
and whether you know it or don't know it, within
its very self nature seeks and strives for God." The
first intention of nature is "the preservation of
the universe" and God loves the entire universe.
"God loves all creatures equally and fills them
with the divine being. And we should lovingly
meet all creatures in the same way." Cosmology is
not value free; it invites our loving response. For

Eckhart, creation is not passive and creation is not something done in the past. In fact, "God created the world in such a way that God is still continually creating it." For "God is life" and "all creatures have an inward divine mode of being." For Eckhart, creation is a grace—he calls creation "the first grace," "gratia gratis data," or, grace gratuitously given. He speaks of "the grace of creation" and "the gift of creation." For what are creatures trying to do? "Each being . . . of the created universe strives, in as much as it is, to cooperate in the assimilation of all things to God." And in this assimilation there is *repose* or rest or delight.

We and all creatures are here to connect to the grace in one another and to the Source of all things. Let us listen with our hearts to Eckhart in the pages that follow as he instructs us further about this holy passage from the inner self to the outer world, from mysticism to prophecy, from loving and listening to the sacred wilderness to preserving it.

The sermons and commentaries in this book are versions of the critical translation in my book *Breakthrough: Meister Eckhart's Creation Spirituality in New Translation,* first published by Doubleday in 1980. Occasionally they have been shortened for this volume. The introductions to the Four Paths are fresh for this volume. When italics are used in the commentaries, this indicates a quote from Eckhart in the sermon that is being discussed. I have chosen to deal with sexist language by using the "he" for God in one sermon and "she" for God in the next sermon, thus alternating genders. It is not a perfect solution to the language problem we have inherited, but at least it acknowledges that there exists a problem.

PATH I

THE VIA POSITIVA

The Via Positiva is our experience of the Divine in delight and wonder, beauty and goodness, awe and amazement. Here the God of light is encountered. Here too the cosmos is experienced as blessing, for human beings do not experience just happiness; we are here to experience *joy*. And there can be no joy in the human realm alone; joy is a gift of the cosmos, a gift of the Spirit who "fills the whole world" as the Book of Wisdom puts it. Recovering a cosmology and a Spirit that fills the cosmos is a necessary part of spiritual awakening. It has everything to do with moving from ego to connectedness, from institutional and superficial relating to an inner life of unfathomable depth.

I met a twenty-seven-year-old a year ago who said to me: "The only mystical experiences I have ever had have been in nature." Eckhart would understand. He says:

All creatures want to express God in all their works; let them all speak, coming as close as they can, they still cannot speak God. Whether they want to or not, whether it is pleasing or painful to them, they all want to speak God and still God remains unspoken.

There exists a tension in creation between expressing God and failing to express God. As much as creatures strive mightily to express the divine, they are not in the long run up to that task, for "the brightness of the divine nature is ineffable. God is a Word but an unexpressed Word." The Word always guards something of the divine silence, the divine mystery. This silence is sometimes painful and sometimes pleasant, but it is always present to creatures, even in the fullest of revelations. (Doesn't every experience of awe contain a suspension of time and noise, i.e., a silence?)

But creation does not get discouraged and does not give up, nor does it operate in vain. In fact, creation is joyful in its efforts to express the divine: "All creatures are gladly doing the best they can to express God." There is a gladness in creation, a joy, a Via Positiva, as each and every creature goes about its task of uttering the divine mystery, of unveiling a unique facet of divine grace and beauty. Every creature is expressing God, that is to say, revealing God. Are we paying attention? Do we treat every creature with the reverence due a source of revelation? Do we treat ourselves that way and recognize how we too are unique revealers of the divine mystery?

Not only are creatures uttering the divine mystery, they are also yearning and striving to experience more of the divine.

CREATION:
A FLOWING OUT
BUT REMAINING
WITHIN

"Preach the Word" (2 TM. 4:2)

The phrase which we read today and tomorrow for the feast of our master, Saint Dominic, comes from Saint Paul's Letter. In the vernacular, it runs this way: Announce the word, pronounce it, produce it, give birth to the word (2 Tm. 4:2).

It is an amazing thing that something flows forth and nonetheless remains within. Words flow forth and yet remain within—that is certainly amazing! All creatures flow outward and nonetheless remain within—that is extremely amazing. What God has given and what God promises to give—that is amazing, inconceivable, and unbelievable. And that is as it should be, for if it were comprehensible and believable things would not be right. God is in all things. The more he is in things, the more he is outside of things. The more he is within, all the more he is without. I have often said God is creating this entire world full and entire in this present now. Everything God created six thousand years ago—and even more —as he made the world, God creates now all at once. God is in everything, but to the extent that God is godly and to the extent that he is intelligible, God is nowhere as much as he is in the soul and also, if you wish, in the angels. He dwells in the innermost dimension of the soul and in the highest aspect of the soul. And when I say "the innermost," I mean the highest. When I say "the highest" I mean the innermost region of the soul. The innermost and the highest realms of the soul —these two are one. There where time never penetrates, where no image shines in, in the innermost and highest aspect of the soul God creates the entire cosmos. Everything which God created six thousand years ago and everything which will be created by God after thousands of years—if the world lasts that long—God is creating all of that in the innermost and highest realms of the soul. Everything which is past and everything which is present and everything which is future God creates in the innermost realms of the soul. Everything which God works in all of his saints, that God works in the innermost realms of the soul. The Father gives birth to his Son in the innermost part of the soul and gives birth to you with his only begotten Son as no less. If I am to be a son then I must be a son in the same being in which the Son exists and in no other being. If I am to be a human being, I cannot have the being of an animal and also be a human being. I must, rather, be a human being in the being of a human person. If I am to be this particular human person then I have to have the existence of this particular human person. Saint John says, "You are children of God" (Jn. 4:4).

"Announce the word, pronounce it, bring it forth, give birth to the word." "Pronounce the word!" What is spoken forth externally and penetrates into you, that is something ordinary. But that word which is spoken inwardly is what we have been discussing. "Pronounce the word"— that means that you should become inwardly one with what is in you. The prophet says: "God spoke one and I heard two" (Ps. 62:11). That is true. God is constantly speaking only one thing. His speaking is one thing. In this one utterance he speaks his Son and at the same time the Holy Spirit and all creatures. And yet there is only one speech in God. The prophet says, "I heard two." That means I heard God and the creature. There where God speaks the creatures, there God is. Here in space and time the creature is. People think God has only become a human being *there* —in his historical incarnation—but that is not so; for God is *here*—in this very place—just as much incarnate as in a human being long ago. And this is why he has become a human being: that he might give birth to you as his only begotten Son, and as no less.

Yesterday I was at a particular place and I spoke a phrase which is in the Our Father: "Let your will be done." It would be better to express this in this way: "Become your will." My will would become your will. I would become your will —that is what the Our Father means. This phrase has two meanings. First, "Be asleep to all things": that means ignore time, creatures, images. The masters say that if a person who is sleeping soundly would sleep for a hundred years, she would forget all creatures, time, and images. And then you could perceive what God works in you.

That is why the soul says in the Song of Songs, "I sleep but my heart watches" (Sg. 5:2). Therefore, if all creatures are asleep in you, you can perceive what God works in you.

Second, this phrase means: "Concern yourself with all things." And this has three meanings. It means, "Take advantage of all things." That means, first, seize God in all things, for God is in all things. Saint Augustine says God has created all things not that he would let them come into existence and then go their own way, but rather he remains in them. People think that they have an advantage if they bring things to God as if God didn't have anything. That is incorrect, for all things added to God are no more than God alone. And if someone who has the Father and the Son with the Father says that he now has more than when he only had the Son without the Father, that would be incorrect. For the Father with the Son is no more than the Son alone. And again the Son with the Father is no more than the Father alone. Therefore, lay hold of God in all things and this will be a sign of your birth, a sign that God has given birth in you himself as his only begotten Son, and nothing less.

The second meaning of "take advantage of all

things" is this: "Love God more than all things
and your neighbor as yourself" (Lk. 10:27). This
is the commandment of God, but, I tell you, it is
not only a commandment. Rather, God has made
us a gift here and has promised to make us a gift.
If you prefer to keep a hundred dollars for yourself rather than giving it to another, that is wrong.
If you love one human being more than another,
that is wrong. If you love your father and mother
and yourself more than another human being,
that is wrong. And if you love your own happiness
more than another's, that is also wrong. "Good
heavens! This can't be right. Should I not love
external happiness for myself more than for another?" There are many learned people who do
not understand this and who find it too difficult.
On the contrary, it is quite easy. I want to show
you that it is not difficult. In each member of the
human body with its particular function, nature
perceives a double goal. The first goal which that
member pursues in its operation is to serve the
body in its totality. And second, each individual
member serves itself and no less than itself.
Within its operations, it doesn't pay any more attention to itself than to another member. How
much more must this be true in the realm of

grace. God ought to be a rule and foundation for your love. The first intention of your love must be oriented purely toward God, and next toward one's neighbor as toward oneself, and no less than toward oneself. If you love beatitude for yourself more than for another you are simply loving yourself. And when you love yourself God is not your pure love, and that is wrong. In effect, if you love the beatitude which is in Saint Peter or in Saint Paul as your own, you possess then the same beatitude which they have for themselves. If you love the happiness of angels as in yourself and if you love the beatitude of our Lady equally with yourself you would enjoy then the same happiness as she does. It belongs to you properly as to her. That is what it says in a book of wisdom: "He has made him equal to his saints" (Si. 45:2).

The third meaning of finding your advantage in all things is this: Love God in all things equally, that is to say, love God as freely in poverty as in riches and look for him in illness as well as in health. Look for him outside of temptation as well as in temptation, in suffering as well as without suffering. The more suffering is great, the more suffering is little, and the more it is like carrying two buckets. The heavier the one, the lighter is the other. The more a person abandons, the easier it will be to abandon. A person who loves God can renounce the entire earth as easily as renouncing an egg. The more one gives, the easier it is to give—as with the Apostles. The heavier their suffering, the easier they were able to support it.

"Apply yourself in all things" means finally that when you find yourself occupied with various things more than with the pure One, test your application. That means "occupy yourself in all things" in view of bringing fulfillment to your service. All of this refers also to the phrase "Lift up your head," and this phrase has two meanings. The first is: Empty yourself of all that is yours and give yourself over to God. Make God to be your own as he is for himself his own, and he will be God for you as he is God for himself, and nothing less. What is truly mine I have received from no one. If I have it from someone else it is not mine, it is hers or his from whom I have it. The second sense of "Lift up your head" is: Direct all your works to God.

There are many people who do not understand this, and this astonishes me. Yet the person who is to understand this must be very detached and elevated above all worldly things. That we should come to this perfection—may God help us.

COMMENTARY

ECKHART'S PANENTHEISTIC THEOLOGY OF
INNESS / WORDS AND CREATURES FLOW OUT
BUT REMAIN WITHIN / THE HIGHEST REGION
OF THE SOUL IS THE INNERMOST PART OF THE
SOUL AND IT IS HERE THAT GOD CREATES /
THE INNER AND OUTER PERSON / GOD AND
CREATION ARE ONE SO WE ARE TO LOVE ALL
THINGS EQUALLY

In this sermon Meister Eckhart expresses his awe at creation's relation to the Creator. He develops a simile of the word that flows out but remains within, comparing all things that exist with the existence of a word. He is *quite amazed* that creatures and words both flow outside their origin and yet remain within that origin. He invites us to explore more in depth the mystery that amazes and which concerns the inness of things. For in the inness of things is God—*God is in all things* he repeats three times in this discourse. He urges us to alter our consciousness and way of seeing things in order to enter into this mystery, telling

us to seize *God in all things, for God is in all things.*
Elsewhere Eckhart urges us to alter our consciousness so as to "bring God down" to where
God truly resides, which is within the inness of
things.

> I reflected tonight that God should be brought
> down, not absolutely, but only within, and so this
> means a God who is brought down. This pleased
> me so well that I wrote it in my book. It runs thus: A
> God who is brought down, not completely, but only
> within, that we may be raised up. That which was
> above came to be within. You shall be united and
> by yourself in yourself, so that He may be within
> you. Not that we take away anything from Him, who
> is above us. We should take into ourselves and
> should take from ourselves into ourselves.

Notice that for Eckhart "bringing God down"
means taking God in. God is not up for Eckhart
and we down. Rather, God is—and wants to be—
in the *innermost* part of us and fully among us.
Divinity dwells on the inside: *When I say the "innermost," I mean the highest*—the innermost becomes
the sublime, *and these two are one.* The in/out dy-
namic that is integral to the motion of creation
also holds for the deepest levels of our spiritual
experience. We can keep God outside by being

too little in touch with our inside and for this reason Eckhart repeats as a constant refrain, and like
a good preacher would, this forgotten but sacred
place: *the innermost part of the soul*. Almost drug-
ging us with this chant to the *innermost part of the
soul,* Eckhart is insisting that we remember it. For
it is here that God creates and that the new creation will be either born or aborted.

But if God is in, we need to get to know the
within. Indeed, if we understood how deeply
within us God dwells, our lives would change.
That is why Eckhart urges us in this sermon to
become aware of what is in you—then we will be
ready to *announce* it, *pronounce* it, *produce* it and
give birth to it. Then our consciousness will change
from thinking two words—God and creatures—to
thinking one word: God. For the Creative Word
has, in the act of creation, only uttered one word
still one more time: *God is constantly speaking only
one thing*. What is that one word? It is God and
creation: *In this one utterance he speaks his Son and at
the same time the Holy Spirit and all creatures*. The
word of God appears as things created here below
and so we imagine that we hear two distinct words
—*God and the creature*. But we need to improve our
hearing. We are to hear just one, we are to hear

creation and listen to the Creator in one act. For God and creation are one utterance. Creation is an expression of divinity, indeed a kind of divinity. Were we more aware of the divinity of our own creation and of what is in us we would know the truth being spoken of. It would be less a surprise and more an experience of Good News.

This theology of inness and this God of the innermost requires a person who is not "out for a walk," as Eckhart puts it. He distinguishes between the outward and the inward person.

> The outward person is the old person, the earthly person, the person of this world, who grows old "from day to day." His end is death . . . The inward man, on the other hand, is the new person, the heavenly person, in whom God shines.

The deep word of God can only be spoken to a person with an inner self. And when it is spoken, unity takes place, for barriers of ego and time, competition and dualism, only exist at the level of superficiality or the outer person's consciousness. *There Time never penetrates* and *no image shines* into the inner person; there God is free to play, to interplay, and to create. Or, as Freud put it, "in the id there is nothing corresponding to the idea of time." Here all creation takes place—*God creates the entire cosmos* and time is suspended so that the eternal is now. And there too the Father begets both the perfect Word and ourselves as the children or words of God. The new creation also takes place at this level of innermost sublimity, where all time stops.

> The inward person is not at all in time or place but is purely and simply in eternity. It is there that God arises, there God is heard, there God is; there God, and God alone, speaks. "Blessed are they that hear the word of God" (Lk. 11:28) there.

Since place as well as time is suspended in this inner depth, the person experiences spacefulness and his or her own greatness.

> There the inward person attains her or his full amplitude *(spatiosissimus est)* because he is great without magnitude. This is the person the apostle commends to us in Colossians (3:10f.): "Putting on the new person which is renewed in the knowledge of God after the image of the One that created us; where there is neither male nor female, Gentile nor Jew . . . barbarian, Scythian, bond or free: but Christ is all and in all."

The word Eckhart uses, *spatiosissimus,* means literally: the most spacious. At this level of inner depth we are most spacious, more without limit, most spacy one might say. We are also most together—at one with the Creator and in the process of becoming a truer and truer image of God and at one with our neighbor irregardless of sex, race, or nation.

Eckhart has not only observed that God is in all things but also that, because of the amazing nature of all creativity, all things are also in their Creator. *All creatures flow outward, and nonetheless remain within.* He elaborates on this understanding of creation and creativity elsewhere:

> When the Father begat all creatures, he begat me also, and I flowed out with all creatures and yet remained in the Father. In the same way, the words that I am now speaking first spring up in me, then secondly I reflect on the idea, and thirdly I express it and you all receive it; yet it really remains in me. In the same way, I have remained in the Father.

Our "remaining in the Father" is an expression of the authentic and altogether orthodox doctrine of panentheism, which means, literally, that all is in God and God is in all. Such a doctrine differs from heterodox pantheism, which means literally "all is God and God is all" and thus disregards the beyondness of God. Indeed, Eckhart

takes special pains in this sermon to demonstrate
that he is not trafficking in pantheism (a charge
that contributed most to his condemnation)
when he indicates that creatures do not add to
God. God is greater than the sum of creation's
parts: *All things added to God are no more than God
alone.* Eckhart's panentheistic theology, which re-
fuses to see God as a Subject or as an Object
outside ourselves or outside creation, is devel-
oped time and time again. He invokes scriptural
evidence for his doctrine: "All things are in God.
'Having all things in thee alone' (Tb. 10:5); 'from
him and through him and in him are all things'
(Rm. 11:36)." "In him we live, move, and have
our being" (Ac. 17:28).

> God created all things, not that they might stand
> outside of himself or alongside of himself or be-
> yond himself, the way other artifacts [made by
> humans] do, but he calls them from nothing, that
> is from nonbeing, so that they may come into and
> receive and dwell in himself. For he is being.

We do not need to ascend to God but to open
our hearts and persons to the truth of how "God
is everywhere and always equally omnipresent."
We ought not to climb up to God, since God is all
around and not up. "As long as we are still in the

ascent we do not attain into him." God, Eckhart declares, is "round-about us completely enveloping us," we are indeed bathed in God as fish who swim in the ocean are bathed in the ocean no less than the ocean bathes in them. "The light embraces all the powers of the soul. Accordingly a master says: 'The light of heaven bathed him.' " For God "is a being that has in itself all being." Elsewhere, Eckhart describes creation as a panentheistic creation, namely as a divine birth within God:

> God created all things in such a way that they are not outside the Godself, as ignorant people falsely imagine. Everything that God creates or does he does or creates in himself, sees or knows in himself, loves in himself. Outside himself he does nothing, knows or loves nothing; and this is peculiar to God himself.

To be unaware of panentheism, of how all beings are in God, is to be "ignorant," Eckhart insists. For things are in God and God is in things. For God this being in and out is no more difficult than it is for the sea that passes through the gills of a fish. *God is in all things. The more he is in things, the more he is outside of things; the more he is within, all the more he is without.* Inside and outside are not opposed for God. We can be inside God and God can be inside us at the same time.

Eckhart warns us not to underestimate what being in God implies. It is a far richer existence than merely being with God and in this sense being in God is deeper than mere friendship wherein friends are *with* one another. For there is implied in being with, a separation and a distance. But being in erases those differences, being in is union and unity. That is why Eckhart, following the Synod of the Council of Reims and Thomas Aquinas as well, can say that "to be in God is to be God." The Word of God came to demonstrate to us how fully in God we were, so fully in God that we too are God's *only begotten Son and no less.* Our becoming God is the very purpose of the Incarnation, which happened in order that *he might give birth to you as his only begotten Son, and as no less.* So like God are we that we become God's will. *I would become your will—that is what the Our Father means.* Our goal is to become as God is—to "be all in all, as God is all in all," as Eckhart puts it elsewhere. Thus we too are to become transparent and panentheistic, bathers and bathed, as God is. And in doing so we experience the same God that God experiences. *God is for himself his own, and he will be God for you as he is God for himself, and nothing less.*

How does this panentheism happen in the everyday world of our lives? It happens in the Mystical Body and in our working to breathe life into new creation. *Direct all your works to God.* It happens by the marriage of word and work: *Announce the word, pronounce it, produce it, give birth to the word!* In the scriptural passage that Eckhart is preaching from we read the following admonition to the builders-up of the mystical body:

> Proclaim the message and, welcome or unwelcome, insist on it. Refute falsehood, correct error, call to obedience—but do all with patience and with the intention of teaching . . . Be careful always to choose the right course; be brave under trials; make the preaching of the Good News your life's work, in thoroughgoing service. (2 Tm. 4:2, 5)

Thus Eckhart addresses himself to the charism of teaching and service of one's lifework, which is preaching the Good News. It is here that he cannot remain silent, even in the moment of his deepest mystical utterances of union of God and creatures, to admonish us to love our neighbor as ourself. Lest the mystically inclined get too carried away with Eckhart's unitive vision and imagine that he is talking of a singular life privately passed with God, he includes the great commandment in this sermon and applies it to a way of living that vivifies the entire mystical body. For if all that is in God is God and if all of creation is in God, then surely we are to *love God in all things equally*. Christ's admonition to love our neighbor as ourself is more than an ethic—it is a way of life that is *not only a commandment* but *a gift* and a way in which we see the world. If we still see self and others as objects or as subjects we still live by commandments only. But if we see the world and its inhabitants as they are—namely in the unity of panentheism—then our actions are ways of *serving the body in its totality*. We have a holistic way of viewing and responding to our neighbor's pain and joy. We begin to act out the truth of what we have grasped: that we are one body, one sole word of God. Furthermore, in loving God we are loving neighbor and vice versa, for our neighbor is in God and God is in neighbor. *Love God more than all things and your neighbor as yourself* (Lk. 10:27). Truly, all creatures do flow outside their origin and yet remain within and this *is certainly amazing.*

SERMON

HOW CREATURES ARE GOD AND HOW GOD BECOMES WHERE CREATURES EXPRESS GOD

"Do not fear those who kill the body but cannot kill the soul." (MT. 10:28)

When God made human beings, God accomplished a deed like to the Godself in the soul—God's masterful deed and God's everlasting deed. This deed was so great that it was nothing other than the soul, and the soul, in turn, was nothing other than God's deed. God's nature, its being, and its Godhead depend on the fact that God *must* be efficacious in the soul. May God be twice blessed! When God is efficacious in the soul, God loves her deed. Now wherever the soul is in which God accomplishes her deed, the deed is so great that this deed is nothing other than love. Again, love is nothing other than God. God loves herself and her nature, her being, and her divinity. In the same love, however, in which God loves herself, she also loves all creatures, not as creatures but she loves the creatures as God. In the same love in which God loves herself, she loves all things.

Now I shall say something I have never said before. God enjoys herself. In the same enjoyment in which God enjoys herself, she enjoys all creatures. With the same enjoyment with which God enjoys herself, she enjoys all creatures, not as creatures, but she enjoys the creatures as God. In the same enjoyment in which God enjoys herself, she enjoys all things.

Now pay attention! All creatures set their course on their highest perfection. Please now perceive what I am about to say, which I swear by my soul is the everlasting truth: I shall repeat what I have never said before: God and the Godhead are as different as heaven and earth. I will go still further: The inner and the outer person are as different as heaven and earth. But God's distance from the Godhead is many thousand miles greater still. God becomes and ceases to become, God waxes and wanes.

Now I shall return to my statement that God enjoys herself in all things. The sun casts its bright light upon all creatures. Whatever the sun casts its light upon draws the sun up into itself; yet as a result the sun does not lose any of its power of illumination.

All creatures want to divest themselves of their *lives* for the sake of their *being*. All creatures are brought into my understanding in that they are spiritually within me. I alone bring all creatures back to God. Look to see how all of you are doing!

Now I shall return to my inner and outer person. I look at the lilies of the field—their bright splendor and their color and all their petals. But I do not see their fragrance. Why is this so? Because the fragrance is in myself. On the other hand, what I say is in myself, and I utter it from within myself. To my outer person all creatures taste like creatures only—like wine and bread and meat. My inner person does not taste things as a creature but rather as a gift of God. My innermost person, however, does not taste a creature as God's gift but rather as something eternal.

I take a basin of water, place a mirror in it, and set it under the sun's orb. The sun then casts its brightness out of its disk and out of its core, and still is not diminished. The reflection of the mirror in the sun is like a sun within the sun, and yet the mirror is what it is. This is the way it is with God. God is in the soul with her nature, her being, and her Godhead, and yet she is not the soul. The reflection of the soul is God in God, and yet the soul is what it is.

God becomes God where all creatures express God: There she becomes "God." When I was still in the core, the soil, the stream, and the source of the Godhead, no one asked me where I wanted to go or what I was doing. There was no one there who might have put such a question to me. But when I flowed out from there, all creatures called out: "God!" I was asked, "Brother Eckhart, when did you go out of the house?" For I had been inside. In this way all creatures speak about "God." And why don't they speak about the Godhead? Everything within the Godhead is unity, and we cannot speak about it. God accomplishes, but the Godhead does not do so and there is no deed within the Godhead. The Godhead never goes searching for a deed. God and the Godhead are distinguished through deeds and a lack of deeds. When I return to "God" and then do not remain there, my breakthrough is more noble than my flowing out. I alone bring all creatures out of their spiritual being into my understanding so that they are one within myself. When I come into the core, the soil, the stream, and the source of the Godhead, no one asks me where I'm coming from or where I've been. No one has missed me in the place where "God" ceases to become.

If anyone has understood this sermon, I wish him well. If no one had been here, I would have had to preach it to this offering box. There are some poor people who will return to their homes and say: "I shall sit down somewhere, eat my loaf of bread, and serve God!" I swear, however, that these people will have to remain in their errors, for they can never attain what these others attain who follow God in poverty and in exile.

ning within and of exiting and entering to
uman experience of the God and Godhead
also to the Creator's experience. Of his own
rience in exiting from his divine origins in
Godhead, Eckhart confesses that only silence
ceded his birth. The Godhead is utterly ineffa-
and there is no talking, no words, in the
odhead: *Everything within the Godhead is unity
nd we cannot speak about it.* But in leaving the
odhead and being born, or as Eckhart puts it
when he *flowed out from there,* all the creatures o
the world could stand up and shout: "God!
Why? Because creatures, on seeing creatures, se
God. In another sermon Eckhart repeats th
same theme. "When I flowed out from God," h
says, "all things spoke: God is." *In this way all cre
tures speak* about "God." God, after all, is th
Creator of creatures. And creatures know, ho
ever dimly it can be remembered, that they spe:
for God. Indeed, they are Bibles and revelatio
about God. "He who knew nothing other th
creatures would have no need for thinking of s
mons, for each creature is full of God and i
book" about God. Humans, too, actually ne
the world in order to know God. "If they co

COMMENTARY

HOW GOD AND GODHEAD DIFFER / HOW GOD
MELTS OUT FROM THE GODHEAD WHEN
CREATION OCCURS / HOW GOD ENJOYS
CREATURES AND WE ARE TO DO THE SAME /
HOW WE LOVE CREATURES AS GOD / THREE
WAYS OF ENJOYING CREATURES

Meister Eckhart sets about exploring more
deeply the creative word or the act of creation by
God. First, he asks the question: What changes
take place in the Creator in the act of creation?
And his response calls upon a theological distinction in understanding the Deity that numer-
ous theologians, including Pseudo-Dionysius,
Thomas Aquinas, Gilbert of Porreta, and others,
made before Eckhart. That is the distinction between God and the Godhead. From our
perspective they are *as different as the earth and the
heavens,* for one operates on earth and the other
remains still in the heavens. The Godhead does
not act—there *are no deeds there.* While God does
act—this is God the Creator who *becomes God where*

all creatures (who are the words of God) express him. God is relative to creation; the Godhead is not. God the Creator is busy in creating things but God the Godhead—who is end as well as beginning—is not busy. "God Himself does not rest where He is the beginning of all being. He rests where He is the end and the beginning of all being."

The distinction between God and Godhead is an effort at the *via negativa,* the God beyond God. The Godhead tradition is an effort to restore the transcendence of the name God to an ineffable Deity. It is also noteworthy that the "Godhead" is feminine gender in both languages in which Eckhart thought. In German it is *Gottheit* and in Latin, *Deitas.* At the same time, the word for "God" is masculine in both languages *(Gott* and *Deus,* respectively). Thus "Godhead" is also an effort to undo an overly masculine gender that a culture and its language have projected onto God —an effort to go beyond the all-male God.

In striving for images of this God beyond God who is the Godhead, Eckhart talks of the deep "ground" out of which the Trinity with its Persons flows. But it is a "hidden" ground, an "abyss," a divine "wasteland." The Godhead is

the "divine God" which is the "n... God. Eckhart is urging his listene... for what one's culture—including c... culture—takes for granted by the of... miliar name of "God." By letting go c... used name for "God" we let God be C... the Godhead emerge. We also allow ou... experience the deep experience of the C...

One might think that human creatio... be capable only of God the Creator. Not ... Eckhart. The human person is so much lik... —Eckhart takes so literally the image of ... theme within the human person—that even... Godhead finds a home there. The human per... is capable of both God and Godhead. Like t... mirror in water that the sun shines upon, *God is i... the soul with his nature, his being, and his Godhead...* And yet Eckhart resists all temptations to confuse ... his teaching with pantheism, for he declares that ... *Yet God is not the soul. The reflection of the soul is God in God, and yet the soul is what it is.* The soul is a mirror of God's beauty and light but it is no more God than is the mirror the sun. These images further delineate Eckhart's panentheism and theology of inness.

Eckhart applies his theme of flowing out and

know God without the world, the world would never have been created for the soul's sake.''

But Eckhart also observes that we are destined to return not only to God but to the Godhead. And when we do, no one will ask any questions, for no one will have missed us. No one is missed in the Godhead, for everyone is there. This return will be even more wondrous, more noble, and more divine than his original flowing out or creation. The return will constitute a genuine breakthrough.

What about God's exit and return? Does God suffer a diminution by becoming a Creator who creates and continually creates and who becomes and not only rests? Eckhart applies the principle of the word that remains within but flows out to God's relationship to the Godhead. God remains ''entirely within herself, not at all outside herself. But when she melts, she melts outwards. Her melting out is her goodness.'' Thus Eckhart uses the image of melting to suggest how things can both go out but remain within and he explains that God's exiting from the Godhead was a thousand-mile journey. God's leave-taking is a melting. Creation is a melting of God's goodness. ''Goodness is present when God melts out and unites with all creatures." The melting and molting that creation is about is thoroughly good. "All creatures have flowed out of God's will . . . All good flows from the superabundance of God's goodness." The key to a worthy love of creatures is never to lose sight of the source of their beauty and goodness—which source is God. "All the good that can exist in creatures—all their honey—is gathered together in God." Eckhart's is not a repressive spiritual psychology but a pleasure-oriented one. He urges us to imbibe in the goodness and "honey-sweetness" of creation instead of standing back to judge it. However, he urges us to enter so fully into creation's beauty, to dive so deep into it, that we get to the source of this goodness who is God. "Creation, and every work of God," he declares, "is perfect as soon as it begins. As Deuteronomy 32 says, 'The works of God are perfect.' " We have nothing to fear from creation. Only from our own shallowness or unwillingness to dive deep into creation where the Creator creates and is always creating. Eckhart's is a spirituality of natural or creation ecstasies: God is truly present in the goodness and honey-sweetness of things and in the experiences of ecstasy we have in communion with such gifts. For if God loves her own melting and therefore savors it in creation and creation in it, then we who are images of God are not forbidden such pleasure either.

Eckhart derives his trust in creation from the Scriptures. The text for the present sermon is as follows:

> Do not be afraid of those who kill the body but cannot kill the soul; fear him rather who can destroy both body and soul in hell. Can you not buy two sparrows for a penny? And yet not one falls to the ground without your Father knowing. Why, every hair on your head has been counted. So there is no need to be afraid; you are worth more than hundreds of sparrows. (Mt. 10:28–31)

The Father or Creator watches over the little things of creation as well as ourselves and there is a trust, a cosmic trust, between Creator and creature. Thus Eckhart reminds us that a *spirit does not kill a spirit. A spirit gives life to the spirit.* What is life-giving—and surely God's Word called creation is such—is not to be feared but trusted, entered into and listened to.

Creation is more than good. Because it is in God, it is God in the sense that we have seen this expression in the previous sermon. The divine relationship between creatures and their Creator is one of intense love on the part of the Creator— love and joy. *In the same love in which God loves herself she also loves all creatures, not as creatures but as God.* God also enjoys all creatures *not as creatures but as God.* Creatures, the words of God, are not only good but divine.

But whether we experience the creatures as they are divine depends on us. We can be puny-minded and timid in our vision like those Eckhart says will return to their house, *sit down somewhere, eat their loaf of bread, and serve God.* Such persons are pitiful, for they settle for so little. They imagine their physical house to be their home whereas in fact God is their home—and not only God but even the Godhead. Why is it that some people settle for so little when there is so much divinity everywhere? It is because they live lives of entertainment of the outer person alone and never bother to explore the inner and then the innermost person. The outer person enjoys the loaf of bread, a glass of wine, and a slice of meat merely as bread, wine, and meat. This way lies boredom. The inner person also enjoys bread, wine, and meat but in that enjoyment does not taste merely the food but also the gift that the food is. Thus the inner person nourishes a sense of gratitude and even wonder at the gift that the ecstasies of creation bless us with. But there is still a third way to experience the gifts of creation. That is the way *of something eternal*. In this tasting, the finiteness of human pleasure is overcome and the grace-filled satisfaction of divine beauty is imbibed. This beauty, the taster knows, will never die. It lasts forever and always tastes delicious.

This analysis of the three levels of consciousness that humans are capable of vis-à-vis creation reveals how for Eckhart the problem with our lives is not our lives but the way we respond to them. We need to pass from mere problem (eating the foods at hand for survival's sake alone) to appreciation and to mystery. As Schürmann puts it, Eckhart "aims at an education of seeing." People who live superficial lives of the outer self alone will never taste eternity in this life—never know what it is to love or to live and thus will always kick at the coming of death, for they will have no firsthand experience that beauty does not die.

So powerful is the consciousness of a person in touch with his or her deepest self that such a person *alone prepares all creatures again for God*. Such a person is capable of a divine act—unifying creation, making cosmos of chaos. *I alone bring all creatures out of their spiritual being into my reason so that they are one within myself.* Such a person knows what God knows: that in God all is one and ought to be one.

Eckhart confesses that, were no one present, he would have been compelled to preach this sermon to the poor box that always stays in church. And, Eckhart confesses, there may be very few who have understood it. Eckhart's humor and capacity to enjoy himself and his work and to laugh at his word, his creation, and his preaching, testify to how free a person he is. He seems to taste of some of the joy and rejoicing that he attributes to God at his creation. If it is true that God *enjoys himself in all things* then Eckhart is trying to practice what he—and God—preach. It is as if Eckhart is not overly attached even to his own work—he lets it flow without, while remaining within—and so, in the last analysis, humor best bespeaks God.

PATH II

THE VIA NEGATIVA

The Via Negativa is the way of experiencing the God of darkness, the God of silence and nothingness, and also the God of suffering. It is a path of letting go and letting be, of emptying and being emptied. It is here especially that Eckhart's teaching parallels much in Zen Buddhism about letting go. Eckhart says: "When all the images of the soul are taken away and the soul can see only the single One, then the pure being of the soul finds passively resting in itself the pure, form-free being of divine unity, when the being of the soul can bear nothing else than the pure unity of God." This implies that Divinity is already present all around us and in us—is this not what Jesus taught when he said "the reign of God is among you"? But we have some work to do in order to see things rightly again, in order to experience the reign of God. That work is essentially a letting-go kind of work, a work of *subtraction*. As Eckhart says, "God is at home; it is we who have gone out for a walk." The work we have to do is a coming-home kind of work, a return to our foundations, to the source of our being and indeed of all being, from which all life and existence gushes up like an unending fountain.

Silence is a wonderful spiritual practice that leads to God's release and our experiencing God. "The most beautiful thing which a person can say about God consists in that person's being silent from the wisdom of an inner wealth. So be silent and do not flap your gums about God." What follows from this letting go of images (for silence is not just audial silence but the silencing of our minds and imaginations as well)?

> I advise you to let your own "being you" sink into and flow away into God's "being God." Then your "you" and God's "his or her" will become so completely one "my" that you will eternally know with God the divine changeless existence and the divine nameless nothingness.

Eckhart points out that we have the capacity to know the Divine and not just know *about* the Divine. The former requires an exercise in *unknowing* or letting go of knowledge.

How should you do this? Without image, without mediation, and without likeness. If I am to know God in such an unmediated way, then I must simply become God and God must become me. I would express it most exactly by saying that God must simply become me and I must become God—so completely one that this "he" and this "I" share one "is" and in this "isness" do one work eternally. For this "he" and this "I"—that is, God and the soul—are very fruitful and they eternally do one work together.

Here Eckhart is describing the union and ecstasy between humans and the divine. The union is not a union for its own sake, but so that a fruitful work occurs from it. Our work is imbued with the strength and beauty and memory of this union. All this happens when we rediscover God in ourselves and the key is to realize that "God is not found in the soul by adding anything, but by a process of subtraction."

Eckhart develops still further—and in a most Zenlike manner—the way of silence and the Via Negativa. He asks:

How then should one love God? You should love God mindlessly, that is, so that your soul is without mind and free from all mental activities, for as long as your soul is operating like a mind, so long does it have images and representations. But as long as it has images, it has intermediaries, and as long as it has intermediaries, it has neither oneness nor simplicity. And therefore your soul should be bare of all mind and should stay there without mind. For if you love God as God is God or mind or person or picture all that must be dropped. How then shall you love God? You should love God as God is—a not-God, not-mind, not-person, not-image—even more, as God is a pure, clear One, separate from all twoness. And we should sink eternally from something to nothing into this One. May God help us to do this.

Eckhart is saying that our soul is not our mind. It is bigger than our mind. It can let go of mind-work and mind-activity and indeed must do so from time to time. We can and must be *bare of all mind and stay there without mind.* Mindlessness precedes mindfulness. Even God needs to be encountered as a "not-God" and a "not-mind, not-person, not-image." We can encounter God one to one; we can be rid of our dualisms between us and God and creatures and God. To do this we need to *sink eternally.* Why eternally? Because the letting go required for experiencing the omnipresence of God never ceases. We sink forever into the Oneness of God, the Oneness of things in God and God in things. Meditation, or the letting go of active imagination and projecting onto God, is an avenue of silence into this way of experiencing God.

But suffering is also a profound part of our spiritual journey, and for Eckhart the proper way to respond to suffering is also the way of the Via Negativa, that of letting be and letting go. We are to let suffering *be* suffering and instead of denial, we ought to "deny denial" and sink eternally into God. We are to enter into the experience of suffering rather than cover it up with addictions or illusions. Life is a series of letting go's—an "infinite" series of letting go's. All things in life are given us "on loan." Stand face-to-face with life, learn to let go, and whatever comes our way—success or failure, joy or sorrow, support or betrayal, light or darkness—it all blesses us. Once we have learned to let go, we are prepared for whatever life gives us. And death itself is nothing to be feared.

How a Radical Letting Go Becomes a True Letting Be

"Blessed are the poor in spirit, for theirs is the kingdom of heaven." (MT. 5:3)

Blessedness opened its mouth of wisdom and spoke: "Blessed are the poor in spirit, for theirs is the kingdom of heaven." Every angel and every saint and everything that was ever born must remain silent when the wisdom of the Father speaks; for all the wisdom of the angels and of all creatures is sheer nothingness before the groundless wisdom of God. And this wisdom has declared that the poor are blessed.

Now there exist two kinds of poverty: an *external* poverty, which is good and is praiseworthy in a person willing to take it upon himself or herself through the love of our Lord Jesus Christ, because he was himself poor on earth. Of this poverty I do not want to speak any further. For there is still another kind of poverty, an *inner* poverty, by which our Lord's word is to be understood when he says: "Blessed are the poor in spirit."

Now I beg you to be just so poor as to understand this speech. For I tell you by the eternal truth, if you are not equal to this truth of which we now want to speak, then you cannot understand me.

Various people have questioned me about what poverty is in itself and what a poor person is. That is what we want to answer.

Bishop Albrecht says that a poor person is one who takes no satisfaction in any of the things that God ever created—and that is well said. But we say it better still and take poverty in a yet higher understanding: he is a poor person who wills nothing and knows nothing and has nothing. Of these three points we are going to speak and I beseech you for the love of God that you understand this truth if you can. But if you do not understand it, do not worry yourselves because of it, for the truth I want to talk about is of such a kind that only a few good people will understand it.

First, we say that one is a poor person who wills nothing. What this means, many people do not correctly understand. These are the people who in penitential exercise and external practices, of which they make a great deal, cling to their selfish I. The Lord have pity upon such people who know so little of the divine truth! Such people are called holy on account of external appearance, but inwardly they are asses, for they do not grasp the real meaning of divine truth. Indeed, these individuals too say that one is a poor person who wills nothing. However, they interpret this to mean that one should so live as to never fulfill one's own will in any way, but rather strive to fulfill the ever-beloved will of God. These people are right in their way, for their intention is good and for that we want to praise them. May God in his mercy grant them the kingdom of heaven. But in all divine truth, I say that these people are not poor people, nor do they resemble poor people. They are highly considered only in the eyes of those who know no better. I, however, say that they are asses who understand nothing of divine truth. Because of their good intentions, they may receive the kingdom of heaven. But of that poverty of which I now want to speak, they know nothing.

These days, if someone asks me what a poor person is who wills nothing, I answer and say: So long as a person has his own wish in him to fulfill even the ever-beloved will of God, if that is still a matter of his will, then this person does not yet possess the poverty of which we want to speak. Indeed, this person then still has a will with which he or she wants to satisfy God's will, and that is not the right poverty. For a human being to possess true poverty, he or she must be as free of his or her created will as they were when they did not yet exist. Thus I say to you in the name of divine truth, as long as you have the will, even the will to fulfill God's will, and as long as you have the desire for eternity and for God, to this very extent you are not properly poor, for the only one who is a poor person is one who wills nothing and desires nothing.

When I still stood in my first cause, there I had no God and was cause of myself. There I willed nothing, I desired nothing, for I was a pure being and a knower of myself in delight of the truth. There I willed myself and nothing else. What I willed, that I was; and what I was, that I willed.

There I stood, free of God and of all things. But when I took leave from this state of free will and received my created being, then I had a God. Indeed, before creatures were, God was not yet "God"; rather, he was what he was. But when creatures came to be and when they received their created being, then God was no longer "God" in himself; rather, he was "God" in the creatures.

Now we say that God, insofar as he is "God," is not a perfect goal for creatures. Indeed, even the lowliest creature *in* God possesses as high a rank. And if a fly possessed reason and could consciously seek the eternal abyss of divine being out of which it has come, then we would say that God, with all he is as God, would still be incapable of fulfilling and satisfying this fly. Therefore we pray God to rid us of "God" so that we may grasp and eternally enjoy the truth where the highest angel and the fly and the soul are equal. There is where I stood and willed what I was, and I was what I willed. So then we say, if people are to be poor in will, they must will and desire as little as they willed and desired when they were not yet. And in this way is a person poor who wills nothing.

Second, a poor person is one who knows noth-

ing. We have said on other occasions that a
person should live a life neither for himself, nor
for the truth, nor for God. But now we say it differently and want to go further and say: Whoever
achieves this poverty must so live that they not
even know themselves to live, either for oneself or
for truth or for God. One must be so free of all
knowledge that he or she does not know or recognize or perceive that God lives in him or her; even
more, one should be free of all knowledge that
lives in him or her. For, when people still stood in
God's eternal being, nothing else lived in them.
What lived there was themselves. Hence we say
that people should be as free of their own knowledge as when they were not yet, letting God
accomplish whatever God wills. People should
stand empty.

Everything that ever came out of God once
stood in pure activity. But the activity proper to
people is to love and to know. It is a moot question, though, in which of these happiness
primarily consists. Some authorities have said that
it lies in knowing, some say it lies in loving, still
others say that it lies in knowing and in loving.
These are closer to the truth. We say, however,
that it lies neither in knowing nor in loving.

Rather, there is a something in the soul from which knowing and loving flow. It does not itself know and love as do the forces of the soul. Whoever comes to know this something knows what happiness consists in. It has neither before nor after, and it is in need of nothing additional, for it can neither gain nor lose. For this very reason it is deprived of understanding that God is acting within it. Moreover, it is that identical self which enjoys itself just as God does. Thus we say that people shall keep themselves free and void so that they neither understand nor know that God works in them. Only thus can people possess poverty. The masters say that God is a being, an intelligent being, and that he knows all things. We say, however: God is neither being nor intelligent nor does he know this or that. Thus God is free of all things, and therefore he is all things. Whoever is to be poor in spirit, then, must be poor of all his own understanding so that he knows nothing about God or creatures or himself. Therefore it is necessary that people desire not to understand or know anything at all of the works of God. In this way is a person able to be poor of one's own understanding.

Third, one is a poor person who has nothing.

Many people have said that perfection consists in people possessing none of the material things of the earth. And indeed, that is certainly true in one sense: when one holds to it intentionally. But this is not the sense that I mean.

I have said before that one is a poor person who does not even will to fulfill God's will, that is, who so lives that he or she is empty both of his own will and of God's will, just as they were when they were not yet. About this poverty we say that it is the highest poverty. Second, we have said one is a poor person who himself understands nothing of God's activity in him or her. When one stands as free of understanding and knowing [as God stands void of all things], then that is the purest poverty. But the third kind of poverty of which we are now going to speak is the most difficult: that people have nothing.

Now give me your undivided attention. I have often said, and great masters say this too: People must be so empty of all things and all works, whether inward or outward, that they can become a proper home for God, wherein God may operate. But now we say it differently. If people stand free of all things, of all creatures, of God and of themselves, but if it still happens that God can find a place for acting in them, then we say: So long as that is so, these persons are not poor in the strictest poverty. For God does not desire that people reserve a place for him to work in. Rather, true poverty of spirit consists in keeping oneself so free of God and of all one's works that if God wants to act in the soul, God himself becomes the place wherein he wants to act—and this God likes to do. For when God finds a person as poor as this, God operates his own work and a person sustains God in him, and God is himself the place of his operation, since God is an agent who acts within himself. Here, in this poverty, people attain the eternal being that they once were, now are, and will eternally remain.

There is a saying of Saint Paul's which reads: "But by the grace of God I am what I am" (1 Co. 15:10). My own saying, in contrast, seems to hold itself above grace and above being and above knowing and above willing and above desiring. How then can Saint Paul's word be true? To this one must respond that Saint Paul's words are true. God's grace was necessarily in him, and the grace of God accomplished in him the growth from accidental into essential being. When grace finished and had completed its work, Paul remained what he was [that is, what he had been before he was].

Thus we say that a person must be so poor that he or she is no place and has no place wherein God could act. Where people still preserve some place in themselves, they preserve distinction. This is why I pray God to rid me of God; for my essential being is above God insofar as we consider God as the origin of creatures. Indeed, in God's own being, where God is raised above all being and all distinctions, there I was myself, there I willed myself, and I knew myself to create this person that I am. Therefore I am cause of myself according to my being, which is eternal, but not according to my becoming, which is temporal. Therefore also I am unborn, and following the way of my unborn being I can never die. Following the way of my unborn being I have always been, I am now, and shall remain eternally. What I am by my [temporal] birth is destined to die and be annihilated, for it is mortal; therefore it must with time pass away. In my [eternal] birth all things were born, and I was cause of myself and of all things. If I had willed it, neither I nor any things would have come to be. And if I myself were not, God would not be either. That God is

"God," of this I am the cause. If I were not, God would not be "God." It is not necessary, however, to understand this.

A great master says that his breakthrough is nobler than his flowing out, and this is true. When I flowed out from God, all things spoke: God is. But this cannot make me happy, for it makes me understand that I am a creature. In the breakthrough, on the other hand, where I stand free of my own will and of the will of God and of all his works and of God himself, there I am above all creatures and am neither God nor creature. Rather, I am what I was and what I shall remain now and forever. Then I receive an impulse which shall bring me above all the angels. In this impulse I receive wealth so vast that God cannot be enough for me in all that makes him God, and with all his divine works. For in this breakthrough I discover that I and God are one. There I am what I was, and I grow neither smaller nor bigger, for there I am an immovable cause that moves all things. Here, then, God finds no place in people, for people achieve with this poverty what they were in eternity and will remain forever. Here God is one with the spirit, and that is the strictest poverty one can find.

If anyone cannot understand this discourse, let them not trouble their hearts about it. For, as long as people do not equal this truth, they will not understand this speech. For this is an unveiled truth that has come immediately from the heart of God.

That we may so live as to experience it eternally, so help us God. Amen.

COMMENTARY

HOW WE ARE TO BECOME FREE OF ALL THINGS
AS GOD IS / EXPERIENCING OUR PREEXISTENCE
IN THE GODHEAD BY ENTERING INTO
NOTHINGNESS / WHY I PRAY GOD TO RID ME OF
GOD / THE MEANING OF LETTING GO AND
LETTING BE / HOW LETTING GO BECOMES
LETTING BE AND REVERENCING ALL THINGS

This sermon is more than a sermon based on
Jesus' Beatitudes from the Sermon on the Mount.
One might even say that it represents Eckhart's
Sermon on the Mount. For he deliberately and
consciously copies the style of Jesus' sayings, as,
for example, when Jesus says, "You *have learned*
how it was said to our ancestors: You must not kill;
and if anyone does kill he must answer for it before the court. *But I say this to you . . .*" This
refrain of "You have learned . . . But I say to
you" is repeated several times in this, Eckhart's
imitation of the Sermon on the Mount. It was
clearly an important sermon in his own estima-
tion since he claims that the truth of it *has come*

immediately from the heart of God and that to grasp it one must have experienced it.

In this sermon Eckhart discusses nothingness. He recalls to our minds what he has said elsewhere, that our origins are *an eternal abyss of divine being* and that *God stands empty of all things* and that *God is free of all things, and therefore he is all things.* Eckhart desires that people too would become so God-like as to touch these states of nothingness that are God's and ours because we are God's images. We too should *stand empty* and should *will nothing, desire nothing, and have nothing.* He wants us to arrive at a point where *God is one with the spirit* and where it happens that *I and God are one.* For it is only this oneness that can give the human person full joy. *Whoever comes to know this something knows what happiness consists in.*

How does one arrive at such oneness and such happiness? It is not enough to travel the cataphatic road to God exclusively. Path One cannot stand by itself because even awareness of our own divinity does not make one happy to one's roots. *When I flowed out from God, all things spoke: God is. But this cannot make me happy, for it makes me understand that I am a creature.* Eckhart seeks to experience our precreaturely state, a time when God was the Godhead and not yet God the Creator, a time before time, a space before place, an eternal youthfulness before aging, a wholeness before brokenness. Eckhart's reflections on this mystical return to the womb before our womb, to our home before home and our God before God are borrowed from wisdom literature, where we read:

> "Yahweh created me when his purpose first
>   unfolded,
>   before the oldest of his works.
> From everlasting I was firmly set,
>   from the beginning, before earth came into
>   being.
> The deep water was not, when I was born,
>   there were no springs to gush with water.
> Before the mountains were settled,
>   before the hills, I came to birth . . .
> I was by his side, a master craftsman,
>   delighting him day after day,
>   ever at play in his presence,
> at play everywhere in the world,
>   delighting to be with the sons of men."
>   (Pr. 8:22–25,30–31)

Eckhart applies these words to Jesus in this sermon, for he says, *Blessedness opened its mouth of wisdom and spoke . . . And this wisdom has declared that the poor are blessed.* Blessedness, as we have seen earlier, means a return to our origins and Eckhart takes the person of Jesus Christ, who *was himself poor on earth,* as a model of what our preexistence must have been back in the Godhead. If it is true, as Eckhart says often, that "Christ is our humanity," and if Christ is an expression of preexisting wisdom, then we too who are called to be other Christs and sons and daughters of God also share in some way in an expression of preexisting wisdom. Back in the Godhead from which we came, *when the wisdom of the Father speaks,* all is silence. We are not then flowing out but only remaining within. It is the exquisite unity with Godhead—this remaining within—that Eckhart invites us to in this sermon. He answers the question: How do we, who are "other Christs" and therefore other wisdoms, set about to be "ever at play in God's presence"? How is the interplay between God and people to happen?

His answer is in terms of poverty. It is poverty that renders us blessed as Jesus, who is *Blessedness* itself, and that renders the kingdom of heaven to happen in our time and where we live. *"Blessed are the poor in spirit, for theirs is the kingdom of heaven."* But Eckhart has a very definite understanding of what he means by poverty. It is *an inner poverty* and a radical poverty. A poverty so radical and so in touch with our ground where Godhead and we

are one, that such a poor person *wills nothing,
knows nothing, and has nothing*. This kind of blessedness and poverty is in touch with nothingness.
Eckhart uses nothingness in four ways: as God
who is no-thing; as our intellects which, like God,
are no-thing; as creatures insofar as they depend
absolutely on God for being and without God are
nonbeing or nothing; and as the transparent way
in which we see through creatures who are nothing into God. All four of these experiences of
nothingness are alluded to in this sermon and are
integral to the truly poor, that is the truly blessed
and happy person.

But how does this happen? Not by a lot of ascetic practices, not by penitences and external
practices which *cling to the selfish I*. Rather, it happens by our learning to let go. Eckhart invented
the words for letting go and letting be. The two
words are *Abgeschiedenheit* and *Gelassenheit* respectively and while some people translate the former
as "detachment," that word has borne too heavy
a burden from dualistic and ascetic spiritualists
since Eckhart's day to do justice to his meaning.
Letting go is what Eckhart means. As Schürmann
puts it, speaking of *Abgeschiedenheit*: This evokes
"a mind that is on the way to dispossession from

all exteriority which might spoil its serenity." The letting go of all things is the act by which we enter into nothingness. "If a person wants to become like God, insofar as a creature can have any likeness to God, then this can only happen through letting go." Letting go allows us to touch nothingness. "Letting go is so near to nothingness, that nothing but God is subtle and rare enough to be contained in letting go." As Caputo puts it, "the object of detachment is 'nothing,' the nothing; indeed, he [Eckhart] says, 'it aims at a pure nothingness.' " Letting go is the virtue behind virtue, the purity behind purity. "Letting go is the best of all, for it purifies the soul and cleans the conscience and inflames the heart and awakens the spirit and enlivens the desires and lets God be known." It is this radical letting go of willing, of knowing, and of having that allows God to enter. "To be empty of all creatures is to be full of God; and to be full of creatures is to be empty of God." The person who has learned to let go is one without objects in his or her life, even life itself is no longer an object. There is true living without why or wherefore. Such a person *must so live that they not even know themselves to live, either for oneself or for truth or for God.*

Furthermore, there are no limits to this kind of poverty, no depths, one might say, to the vortex that is our spirit and our potential for letting go and for nothingness. One might say that nothing is the limit to letting go or, if you will, God is the limit. For so radical is Eckhart's invitation to let go that he confesses twice in this sermon that he prays to God to *rid us of God*. Why does he do this? *This is why I pray God to rid me of God; for my essential being is above God insofar as we comprehend God as the origin of creatures.* In other words, believing he is capable of the Godhead and not only of God, he prays to let go of our images for God—even for the Creator God. And of our will for God. To experience the true Godhead where all creation exists now as earlier and now as in the future, it is necessary to be rid of all—including our names for God. We need to let go of all our works as well in order that God might work. We are to keep ourselves *so free of God and of all one's works that if God wants to act in the soul, God himself becomes the place wherein he wants to act—and this God likes to do.* Full emptiness is required, or true poverty. He alludes to this same letting go of God on other occasions:

The highest and loftiest thing that a person can let go of is to let go of God for the sake of God. When Saint Paul let God go for the sake of God, he let everything go that he could get from God, and he let everything go that God could give him and he let everything go that he could receive from God. When he let go of all this, he let God go for the sake of God and then God remained with him where God is most truly in himself . . . He did not give anything to God, nor did he receive anything from God, for he and God were one unity and one pure union.

The allusion to Saint Paul is from Romans, where we read:

What I want to say now is no pretense; I say it in union with Christ—it is the truth—my conscience in union with the Holy Spirit assures me of it too. What I want to say is this: my sorrow is so great, my mental anguish so endless, I would willingly be condemned and be cut off from Christ if it could help my brothers of Israel, my own flesh and blood. (Rm. 9:1–4)

It is here—in Paul's willingness to be "cut off from Christ"—that Eckhart derived his concept of *Abgeschiedenheit* (from the word "to cut off") and letting go even of God. He explains this elsewhere: "Saint Paul says that he would like to renounce God for the sake of God, in order that the glory of God might be extended." It is significant that Eckhart invokes Paul in the present sermon as an example of someone whom God favored. *Paul's words are true. God's grace was necessarily in him, and the grace of God accomplished in him the growth from accidental into essential being.* In Eckhart's scriptural text for this verse from Romans, the word Paul uses that expresses his being cut off even from Christ is *geschieden*. This, then, is a major biblical text for Eckhart's teaching of a path of letting go.

The purpose of letting go is not to renounce things as bad or immoral or even to forget things. If that were the case, then Eckhart's admonition to let go of God would be tantamount to repressing God. The purpose of the *via negativa* and the experience of the apophatic God or God of nothingness is not to put down or to forget the God of creation. In Eckhart's journey, Path Two does not stand by itself. Nor does it substitute for Path One. The purpose of letting go is to experience the divinity in all creation to an even greater depth. "He who has God essentially apprehends God in a godly manner, and to such a person God

shines in all things, for all things have a divine
savor for him, and God becomes visible for him in
all things.'' In fact, letting go lets us see the divinity behind the divinity of things. "This person is
highly praised before God because he perceives
all things in a godly manner and values them
more than the things are worth in themselves.''

Thus the ultimate experience of letting go is
an experience of letting be. Letting God be God
and letting the Godhead be the Godhead. Letting
oneself be oneself and letting others be themselves. Letting things be things and letting God be
God in things and things be God in God. Letting
inness be and letting panentheism be and letting
the circle of being that God surrounds be.
Schürmann puts it this way: "As existence moves
ahead on this road [of *Abgeschiedenheit*], all ascetic
imperatives vanish. Thus detachment turns pro-
gressively into releasement, *Gelassenheit*, which, as
has been said, is a broader concept." Letting be
or *Gelassenheit* comes from the word *lassen*, to let
go, to relinquish or abandon. It also means to allow or permit. Thus, says Caputo, "it suggests
openness and receptivity." It is a state of being
open and sensitive. It means, says Eckhart, to be
"receptive of all spirit.''

Our Lord speaks very clearly: "Blessed are the poor in spirit." He who has nothing is poor. "Poor in spirit" means that, as the eye is poor and bare of color and yet receptive of all colors, in the same way the person who is poor in spirit is receptive of all spirit, and the spirit of all spirits is God.

Thus what letting go does is to develop sensitivity and openness to the spirit and this receptivity results in letting be. Schürmann describes letting be as an act of respecting the autonomy of things. "It designates the attitude of a human who no longer regards objects and events according to their usefulness, but who accepts them in their autonomy." Thus a good synonym for letting be might be reverence. Letting be is an attitude of reverence for all things that allows them to be themselves and God's selves. This represents one more reason why the path of letting go and letting be is not one of putting down anything or any event. It is rather to enter so fully into events and things that we reverence all that is there. This reverence is a gentle letting be. "What is being spoken of here is to meet with gentleness, in true humility and selflessness, everything which comes your way." Such an attitude of reverence and letting be actually forbids our running away from things and requires our return to them to see them newly. As Caputo puts it:

> the detached man in Meister Eckhart is not simply to be understood as one who has divested himself of all self-love, but also as one who, like Martha, is at home in the world of things, who has a new relationship to creatures, who understands them for what they are, who lets them be.

Thus Meister Eckhart can say:

> One cannot learn this [to perceive God in all things] by flight, by fleeing from things, and from externality to solitude, but one must learn to cultivate an inward solitude, wherever or with whomsoever one may be. One must learn to break through things and to grasp one's God in them and to be able to picture him powerfully to oneself in an essential manner.

Thus letting go and letting be are about a *return* to creation, not a flight from it. They are our way of seeing creation newly, which actually means the way it is and originally was and was always intended to be, namely, in God.

In this blessed and new creation, where letting go and letting be result in reverence even for nothingness in all its forms, the *groundless wisdom of God* is allowed to speak once again. It will speak with the word that no one has heard since before they were born. It will utter a word of silence and unity that only silence can shout of. It will not be an abstract or a distant silence, however, but one that accompanies all of our activities. This attitude of utter reverence and gentle receptivity we are to bring to all we do, advises Eckhart, even to the sermon that he speaks. *If you are not equal to this truth of which we now want to speak, then you cannot understand me.* This is the *gentle and receptive silence that precedes all understanding.* By traveling this path we shall return to the God before God, to the space and time where *God was not yet "God,"* that is, to the Godhead who was God before creation. And there we shall be free—as free as God is—to play "by his side . . . delighting him day after day, ever at play in his presence, at play everywhere in the world." There we will come to know the *something in the soul,* the spark of our souls and our touch of divinity *from which knowing and loving flow.* And there, in the unity of our origins with God, joy will not cease. *Whoever comes to know this something knows what happiness consists in.* There all barriers will break down; we will no longer be a people who *preserve distinctions.* We will be one in God and God in us so that, like

Paul, we will remain what we are and what we have been from all eternity. For when the distinction between God and us is let go of and allowed to break down, then too the distinction between existence and preexistence gives way. Time no longer holds power over us. We become, in the Godhead's presence, eternally at play. *Here God is one with the spirit.*

PATH III

THE VIA CREATIVA

The Via Creativa is about experiencing the divine in the act of creativity, in the holy act of giving birth. Since we are images of the "Artist of artists" as Thomas Aquinas calls God, we are all artists in some way. We all have images to give birth to and we are here to assist one another as midwives do at the time of birth. Meister Eckhart, who in the Via Negativa has emphasized our being empty or "virginal," nevertheless praises our giving birth as being of even deeper importance.

> The word *wife* is the noblest term that we can attribute to the soul; it is far nobler than *virgin*. It is good for a person to receive God into oneself, and in this receptivity he or she is a virgin. But it is better for God to become fruitful within the person. This is because becoming fruitful as a result of the gift is the only gratitude for the gift. . . . A virgin who is a wife, and who is free and liberated and without ego attachment, is always equally close to God and herself. She bears much fruit, and the fruit is of

good size. It is no less nor more than the Godself. This virgin who is a wife bears this fruit and this birth. Every day she bears fruit a hundred times or a thousand times or countless times giving birth and becoming fruitful out of the most noble foundation of all. Let me put it in even a better way. Indeed, she bears out of the same foundation from which the Father begets his eternal Word and from which she becomes fruitfully pregnant.

In this passage Eckhart is underscoring how deep prayer—that of gratitude for life—is synonymous with our creativity. "Becoming fruitful as a result of the gift is the only gratitude for the gift." When we give our gift we are giving the gift of the Cosmic Christ, that is to say, "it is no less nor more than the Godself." This is something we can do on a daily basis, this giving of our gift. And where does the gift come from? From "the most noble foundation of all," from the very same foundation where God begets the divine Son and where the Holy Spirit makes us all pregnant with new creation as it did for Mary, the mother of Jesus. Art as meditation is a prayer form that brings the Trinity to our lives and our culture. It brings the divine alive.

Eckhart reminds us of maternal as well as paternal images of Divinity when he says the following:

> God from all eternity has given birth to the divinely begotten Son and continues to give him birth now and into all future eternities—so teaches a master—and so God lies in the maternity bed, like a woman who has given birth, in every good soul which has abandoned its self-centeredness and received the indwelling God. . . .
>
> A master says that he thinks now and then on the words the angel spoke to Mary: "Hail, full of grace" (Lk. 8:21). What help is it to me that Mary is full of grace if I am not also full of grace? And what help is it to me that the Father gives birth to his Son unless I too give birth to him? It is for this reason that God gives birth to his Son in a perfect soul and lies in the maternity bed so that he can give birth to him again in all his works.

Here Eckhart challenges us to do what Mary did: give birth to the divine son or daughter in us. To give birth to the Cosmic Christ that is uniquely ours to give birth to. It is in our "souls," that is to say in our innermost depths, where creativity springs from, that such birth takes place. Our souls *are* the divine maternity bed.

BE YOU CREATIVE
AS GOD IS CREATIVE

*"It is all that is good, everything that is perfect,
which is given us from above."* (JM. 1:17)

Saint James says in his Epistle: "The best gift and
perfection come from on high from the Father of
lights" (Jm. 1:17).

Saint James speaks of "every gift." Now the
best of all and the highest of all are really gifts in
the most proper meaning of the term. God gives
away nothing so happily as big gifts. I stated once
in this place that God prefers to forgive big sins
rather than small ones. And the bigger they are,
the more happily and quickly does God forgive
them. This is quite the way it is with grace and
gifts and virtues: the bigger they are, the more
happily does God give them. For it is God's nature
to give big gifts. And for this reason, the more
valuable the gifts are, the more does Divinity give

of them. The most noble creatures are the angels, who are purely spiritual and have nothing corporeal about them. There are a very great many of them, and there are more of them than the sum total of all corporeal things. Big things are called quite properly "gifts" and belong to God in the truest and most spiritual way.

I once said that whatever can be truly expressed in its proper meaning must emerge from inside a person and pass through the inner form. It cannot come from outside to inside of a person but must emerge from within. It lives truly in the most spiritual part of the soul. There all things are present, living and seeking within the soul what is spiritual, where they are in their best and highest meaning. Why don't you notice anything of this? Because you are not at home there. The more noble something is, the commoner it is. I have my senses in common with the animals, and my life in common with the trees. My being, which is more inward, is held in common with all creatures. Heaven is more encompassing than all that is under it, and for this reason it is more noble. Love is noble because it is all-encompassing.

What our Lord has commanded seems difficult—that we should love our fellow Christian like ourselves (Mk. 12:31; Mt. 22:39). Coarse people commonly say that the meaning of this is that we should love our fellow Christians with a view to the same benefit for the sake of which we love ourselves. No, this is not the case. We should love them just as much as ourselves, and that is not difficult. If you wish to think correctly on this matter, love is more of a reward than a command. A command sounds difficult but a reward is something to long for. All of us who love God as we should and must love God, whether willingly or not, and the way all creatures love God, must love our fellow human beings like ourselves. We must rejoice in their joys as much as in our own joys, we must long for their honor as much as for our own honor, and we must love a stranger as our own relatives. In this way, people are constantly in joy and honor, and a good situation, just as if they were in the kingdom of heaven. Thus they have more frequent joys than if they only had joy in their own benefits. And know for certain that, if your own honor causes more happiness than the honor of another, something is wrong.

Know that, whenever you are seeking your own interest, you will never find God, since you are not seeking God alone. You are looking for something along with God, and you are behaving exactly as if you were making of God a candle so that you could look for something. When we find the things we are looking for, we throw the candle away. Whatever you are seeking along with God is *nothing*. It does not matter what it is—be it an advantage or a reward or a kind of spirituality or whatever else—you are seeking a *nothingness*, and for this reason you find a *nothingness*. The reason that you find a *nothingness* is that you are seeking a *nothingness*. All creatures are a pure *nothingness*. I do not say that they are of little value or that they are something at all—they are a pure *nothingness*. Whatever has no being is nothing. All creatures lack being, for their being depends on the presence of God. If God were to turn away from all creatures only for a moment, they would come to nothing. I have from time to time made a statement that is also true: whoever added the whole world to God would have nothing more than if she had taken God by herself. All creatures have, without God, no more being than a gnat would possess without God—just exactly as much and not less or more.

All right, now listen to a true statement! If a person gave a thousand gold marks so that churches and monasteries could be built, this would be a fine thing. All the same, if another person who regarded a thousand marks as nothing gave much more, the second donor would have done more than the first one. When God created all the creatures, they were so unimportant and narrow that she could not move about in them. She made the soul, however, so like and similar in appearance to herself that she could give herself to the soul. For what she gave to the soul in addition is regarded by the soul as nothing. God must give herself to me just as much as she belongs to herself, or there will be no advantage to me at all, and nothing will agree with me. Any people who are to receive her so completely must give themselves up completely and be completely divested of themselves. Such people receive from God all God has and as much as our Lady and all those in heaven have. All of this belongs to these people in a similar and quite personal way. Those who have divested themselves of themselves to the same degree and have surrendered themselves will receive the same from God and no less.

And now let us consider the third part of our text from the Scripture: "from the Father of the

light." The word "Father" makes us think of son-
ship or daughtership; the word "Father" signifies
a pure generation and means the same as "a life
of all things." The Father generates his Son in
eternal knowledge. She generates her Son in the
soul exactly as in her own nature. She generates
him in the soul as her own, and her being is attached to the fact that she is generating her Son
in the soul, whether for good or for woe. I was
once asked what the Father did in heaven. And I
said that she was generating her Son, and that this
activity was so agreeable to her and pleased God
so much that she does nothing other than generate her Son, and both of them flourished in the
Holy Spirit. When the Father generates her Son
in me, I am that very same Son and no one else.
"If we are sons and daughters, we are heirs as
well" (Rm. 8:17). Whoever rightly knows the
truth understands well that the word "Father"
implies a pure generation and a production of
children. For this reason we are here as a child,
and are the same Son.

Now note also the expression: "They come
from above." I recently told you that whoever
wishes to receive something from above must of
necessity be below in proper humility. And know

in the truth that whoever is not fully below will receive nothing, however insignificant it might ever be. If you have ever perceived this with respect to yourself or something else or someone else, then you are not down below and you will receive nothing. If you are really below, you will receive fully and completely. It is God's nature to make gifts, and her being depends on making gifts to us if we are down below. If we are not here, and if we receive nothing, we act violently toward God and we kill God. If we cannot do this to God, we are still doing it to ourselves and being violent as far as we are concerned. See to it that you give everything to God as her own, and that you humble yourself beneath God in proper humility, and that you raise up God in your heart and your perception. "God, our Lord, sent her Son into the world" (Ga. 4:4). I said once at this point that God sent her Son in the fullness of time—to our soul, if it has moved beyond all time. If the soul is unencumbered by time and space, the Father sends her Son into the soul. Now this is the meaning of the declaration: "The best gift and perfection come from on high from the Father of lights."

May the Father of lights help us to be ready to receive God's best gift! Amen.

COMMENTARY

THE CREATOR AS ARTIST, THE SON AS ART /
ECKHART'S THEOLOGY OF CREATIVITY AND THE
ARTIST / BECAUSE IT IS GOD'S NATURE TO GIVE
GIFTS, IT IS OURS ALSO / OUR BEST GIFTS OR
WORKS OF ART COME FROM WITHIN AND THUS
PRAISE GOD / OUR DIVINE DESTINY AND GLORY
IS TO RECEIVE BEAUTY AND BIRTH BEAUTY—
AND THIS IS SALVATION

It has been said that one can "extract an almost
complete philosophy of art from Eckhart's writ-
ings," and that is true. This would seem to be
demonstrated by the journey we have taken thus
far. Through Path One we experienced the divine
isness of all creation, so full of divine beauty
planted there by an Artist. Through Path Two we
learned to let go in order to let the beauty be. In
Path Three we learn that we are to be parents of
the Beauty behind beauty and the Artist behind
artists and that the Holy Spirit, spirit of gift-giving,
inspires us to birth gifts. In the present sermon
Eckhart, drawing on scriptural passages from

James and Paul, summarizes the culmination of
Path Three in the spiritual journey as an experience of birthing and creativity. Each of these
epistles speaks of our vocation as children of God
and "first-fruits" of the Creator's work. Thus the
passage from James that forms the starting point
for Eckhart's sermon reads:

> Make no mistake about this, my dear brothers: it is
> all that is good, everything that is perfect, which is
> given us from above; it comes down from the Fa-
> ther of all light; with him there is no such thing as
> alteration, no shadow of a change. By his own
> choice he made us his children by the message of
> the truth so that we should be a sort of first-fruits of
> all that he had created. (Jm. 1:16–18)

This reiteration of creation as a blessing and of
the human race as the first-fruits of creation, a
special blessing that makes us children of God, is
a theme that Eckhart is pleased to treat. To explore more deeply the meaning of our son/
daughtership to God, Eckhart invokes two passages from Paul's epistles. Each talks of not only
the gift of being divine children but also the responsibility. We are heirs as well as God's sons and
daughters, and we possess "the first-fruits of the
spirit."

Everyone moved by the Spirit is a son of God. The spirit you received is not the spirit of slaves bringing fear into your lives again; it is the spirit of sons, and it makes us cry out, "Abba, Father!" The Spirit himself and our spirit bear united witness that we are children of God. And if we are children we are heirs as well: heirs of God and coheirs with Christ, sharing his sufferings so as to share his glory . . . From the beginning till now the entire creation, as we know, has been groaning in one great act of giving birth; and not only creation, but all of us who possess the first-fruits of the Spirit, we too groan inwardly as we wait for our bodies to be set free. (Rm. 8:14–17,22,23)

Eckhart comments on this passage: *When the Father generates his Son in me, I am that very same Son and no one else . . . We are here as a child, and are the same Son.* He turns to Galatians to reinforce his point, emphasizing our passage from being heirs to being sons:

An heir, even if he has actually inherited everything, is no different from a slave for as long as he remains a child. . . . The proof that you are sons is that God has sent the Spirit of his Son into our hearts: the Spirit that cries, "Abba, Father," and it is this that makes you a son, you are not a slave anymore; and if God has made you son, then he has made you heir. (Ga. 4:1,6–7)

Eckhart interprets our coming of age as our receiving God in our souls. *God sent his Son in the fullness of time—to our soul, if it has moved beyond all time. If the soul is unencumbered by time and space, the Father sends his Son into the soul.* And this sending constitutes *"the best gift and perfection come from on high from the Father of lights."* It also constitutes our motherhood of God and our becoming Creators as God the Father is.

> Nevertheless, it does not suffice for the noble, humble person to be the only begotten Son, whom the Father has eternally begotten, unless he or she also wants to be a father and to enter this similitude of the eternal Fatherhood, and to beget him by whom I am eternally begotten.

Eckhart devotes considerable energy in this sermon to exploring what "Abba, Father" might mean. Who is this God who is addressed as "Abba, Father"? God is a being driven to generate or give birth. God is *pure generation* and is the *life of all things.* The essence of God is to give birth. *The word "Father" signifies a pure generation and means the same as "a life of all things."* That which the Father most generates is his Son, and this birthing is a constant birthing process.

> I was once asked what the Father did in heaven. And I said that she was generating her Son, and that this activity was so agreeable to her and pleased her so much that she does nothing other than generate her Son, and both of them flourished in the Holy Spirit.

Birthing the Son is God's constant activity. This is what is meant when we call out, "Abba, Father." *The word "Father" implies a pure generation and a production of children.* This generating is not restricted to a far-off place called heaven. It actually takes place in ourselves. *She generates her Son in the soul exactly as in her own nature. She generates him in the soul as God's own, and her being is attached to the fact that she is generating her Son in the soul, whether for good or for woe.* But this generating that God does in us is also what the indwelling of God in us is about. "Her generating is at the same time her indwelling, and her indwelling is her generating." Thus for Eckhart the indwelling of God is meant to be fruitful and outward-oriented. It is not an inner symbol to gaze at so much as an inner dynamism that is to generate our own creativity and giving birth. Contemplation is not a rest in God but a flowing out from God into birthing. What God generates and gives birth to is ourselves as the Son of God. *Where the Creator generates her Son in me, I am that very same Son and no one else.*

We are sons and daughters of the Father! But to be children of the Father who is *pure generation* means that we too are to generate, we too are to be birthers who are divinely fruitful. This is our praise of God, namely our creativity.

> What praises God? That which is like God. Thus, everything in the soul which is like God praises God. Whatever is at all unlike God does not praise God. In the same way, a statue praises the artist who has imprinted on it all the art that he has in his mind, thus making it so very like his conception. The similarity of the work of art to the artist's conception praises the master without words.

By discovering how we are artists as God is, we praise God, who in fact intended that we be in his image and likeness and therefore creators also. Elsewhere Eckhart explains that the Father and the Son are related as is the artist to his or her art. Art stays with the artist like the Word stays with the Father. It flows out but remains within. Eckhart links in an explicit way his theology of creativity with his theology of the Word.

> From the start, once she has become an artist and as long as she is an artist capable of creative work, art remains with the artist. This is the meaning of "The Word was in the beginning with God," that is, the art with the artist, coeval with him, as the Son is with the Father in God.

God's Word is God's work. It goes out but remains within. The same is true of us. "What is in me goes out from me; if I am only thinking it, then my word reveals it and yet remains inside me. It is in this way that the Father speaks the unspoken Son and yet the Son remains in the Father." Since we too are God's children, it follows that we too are God's works of art. But also, being heirs of God come of age, we too are artists as God is. To be a human being as well as to be a divine being means that we are artists, for "humankind lives by art and reason, that is to say, practically." We are heirs of God, heirs of creativity. We are heirs of the "fearful creative power" of God.

Psychologist Otto Rank has defined the artist as one who wants to leave behind a gift. Integral to an artist's consciousness is a gift-consciousness, a thank you for creation that is expressed in one's creativity. Eckhart's is a theology of thanksgiving. His theology of the Spirit is a theology of gift-giving, for the Spirit is a gift. In the present sermon Eckhart develops in a richer way how it is that God's consciousness is a gift-consciousness and therefore, using Rank's criterion, a consciousness of the artist. God needs to make gifts, Eckhart says. God is, as it were, compelled to be an artist. *It is God's nature to make gifts, and God's being depends on making gifts to us if we are down below.* So important is this gift-giving to God's nature that if we refuse the gift, *we act violently toward God and we kill God.* In other words, a gift-giver requires a gift-receiver, as every artist requires an audience and a union with others. To refuse God that audience is to challenge the very core of God, for if it is her *nature* to give gifts, then truly *her being depends on it.*

What kind of gifts does God like to give? The bigger, the better. *God gives away nothing so happily as big gifts . . . It is her nature to give big gifts.* Notice that this gift-giving is a *giving away.* It is not a giving for a return or a reward. It is a giving in order to give, it is gift for gift's sake, it is giving without a why. As Eckhart puts it, we even make God into a means as we do a candle. Then, *when we find the things we are looking for, we throw the candle away.* God must be an end and a mystery, not merely a means or a problem-solver in our lives. So too, all our gift-giving and thank-you's, all our art, are to be without a why like living and work. Art is without a why just like creation itself. In another sermon Eckhart had warned us that "those who give in order to receive something in return" are not giving gifts. "Such a gift does not deserve to be called a gift; it should be called a demand because nothing is really given." God is always ready with his gifts, but we often miss the opportunity. "As exalted as God is above human beings, to that same extent is God more prepared to give than human beings are to receive." The most basic of the gifts we have received is of course being itself. This we have in common with all creatures and because of this gift *all creatures love God* (see Path One). So basic is being that even our art or gift-giving depends on it. "Each and every thing, whether produced by nature or by art, has its being or the fact that it is immediately from God alone." The intimacy we share with God the giver of being is shared by all our art as well and all we give birth to. The greatest of the gifts we have received is the Son and we are driven to respond with what Schürmann calls a "supreme thankfulness":

> The reception of God . . . in us is a gift which must bear fruit: detachment is completed by fertility . . . one sole determination joins them [people and God] together: that of giving birth. United to God in begetting, man returns to God in an act of supreme thankfulness everything that he possesses.

If it is God's nature to give gifts—and preferably big ones—then it is our nature as sons and daughters of God to do the same. Our divinization requires our creativity. One cannot be divine without being creative and fruitful.

What does it mean to be creative and to be an artist for Eckhart? It means to give birth from the very depths of our insides. It means being in touch with and being ready to express the inner and not the outer person.

> Whatever can be truly expressed in its proper meaning must emerge from inside a person and pass through the inner form. It cannot come from outside to inside of a person, but must emerge from within.

Introvert meditation—the taking in of a symbol given from the outside—is not enough for Eckhart. We need extrovert meditation as well—one that expresses our own deepest insides. Being and action are united deep inside us. Thus our act of creativity must flow from our act of being. The culmination of the birth of God and us will be a creativity that is itself born of being and action, the way God's is. All creatures, Eckhart declares, "strive in their works toward what is like their own being." We are urged to "bear fruit that remains" (Jn. 15:16), but it is what is deepest in us that remains. "What is inborn in me remains." What is deep within the artist are images that are more than images—they are life itself—flowing out but remaining within, as does a word.

> The chest which issues or is produced externally into being nevertheless is and remains in the artist himself, just as it was from the beginning, before it became a chest . . . The chest in the mind and art of the artist is neither a chest nor is it made, but is art itself, is life, the living concept of the artist.

Art, like life, is born from our deepest roots and centers. For art is life.

> What is life? That which is moved by itself from within. What is moved from without does not live. Hence, if we live with God, we must also cooperate with God from within, so that we do not operate

> from outside; we should rather be moved from
> whence we live, that is, through God. Now we can
> and must act from our own, from within. If, there-
> fore, we shall live in God or by her, she must be our
> own and we must act from our own . . .

Eckhart is hopeful—we "can operate from within"—that we can all be artists and creative people in some way. Indeed, we must be, for this is the only route in which authentic pleasure lies. *God's being requires her to wish what is best . . . If you love your God, nothing could give you more pleasure than whatever pleases God best.* Our greatest pleasure is in cooperating with the Creator, creator with Creator, artist with Artist. Every artist has experienced the ecstasy of "enchantment" that Eckhart speaks of for those who become instruments of the divine creativity. In the creative state, "the soul now no longer accomplishes things with grace but divinely in God. Thus the soul is in a wonderful way enchanted and loses itself." To experience this ecstasy and pleasure that art brings, we need to trust our images as God does. The artist is driven to trusting her own images and concepts, to operating from within outward. True art is always from our depths to others' depths, a gift or a spirit that touches other spirits and flows from within to within. So committed must the artist be to trusting his or her images that the artist must actually become one being with the image and live for the image. "An image receives its being immediately from that of which it is an image. It has one being with it and it is the same being." Our life with our images—our artistic life—becomes a pattern for our spiritual lives. "You often ask how you should live. Note this carefully. See what has just been said of the image. In exactly the same way, you should live. You should be in God and for God, and not in yourself and for yourself." The trust and spontaneity of the artist become models for our spiritual lives.

> Human beings should turn their will to God in all their activities and keep their eyes on God alone, marching along without fear and without hesitancy about being right or not doing anything wrong. For if a painter wanted to consider every stroke of her brush when she made his first stroke, no picture would ever result . . . This is why we should follow the first suggestion and move forward.

The reason the artist must plumb his or her inner life more than others is that there is where the action takes place. All things are present there. *There all things are present, living and seeking within the soul what is spiritual, where they are in their best and highest meaning.* The reason we do not grasp this is that we are strangers to our own capacity to give birth and to imagine images. *Why don't you notice anything of this? Because you are not at home there.*

The work of finding the transcendent within is the work that the Holy Spirit accomplished in Mary's birth of Jesus, Eckhart says. Every artist must make what is "above" be "within."

> The work that is "with," "outside," and "above" the artist must become the work that is "in" her, taking form within her, in other words, to the end that she may produce a work of art, in accordance with the verse "The Holy Spirit shall come upon thee" (Lk. 1:35), that is, so that the "above" may become "in."

Once again Eckhart is relating his theology of creativity to his theology of the Spirit and to his theology of birthing. The fruit of our birthing from within, instead of merely from outside or even from above, will be God-with-us, Emmanuel, still another birth of God in our midst. In this sense, Mary was the first folk artist, the first one to birth God from within and not merely from without or above. Mary had the imagination, the courage, and the discipline to make the most sublime the innermost. To bring God *in* and to birth God outwardly. This is what is so noble and divine about the "intellect," or what I prefer to call the imagination in us, the *imago Dei*.

But imagination does not come from wishing or fantasizing alone. Eckhart distinguishes two kinds of willpower within us: that which is merely wishing and which is not born deeply from within, and that which is "determining and creative" and which is truly a will to create. The latter is only tapped if we give birth from deep within us, as every true artist must. Art is not mere inspiration. It takes an act of the will and a willingness to discipline oneself. Thus it calls upon qualities of a person that mere wishing to be an artist does not; it calls upon inner discipline. "The artist does not find his nature sufficient for the practice of his art unless it is reinforced by the will to practice it, the capacity and the skill and so on, factors which are not, strictly speaking, the nature of the artist." Clearly Eckhart prefers this kind of discipline to that of ascetic mortifications, for it is oriented toward bearing fruit and not just being a contemplative "virgin."

The journey that the artist makes in turning

inward to listen to and trust his or her images is a communal journey. Jungians say that there is a collective unconscious. Eckhart puts it in the following manner. *My being, which is more inward, is held in common with all creatures.* The more outward we look at things, the more separately we see them. We have *senses in common with the animals, life in common with the trees.* But that which is in common with all other creatures, our being, is *more inward.* Thus the artist who is truly birthing from the depths of the inside is birthing from the depths of commonality. Such a person is giving birth to the "we" and not just the I. In fact, Eckhart wants to do away with the word "I":

> The word *ego,* which means "I," is appropriate only for God in his unity. The word *vos* means approximately "you." That fact that you are one in unity means that the words *ego* and *vos* ("I" and "you") point to unity. May God help us to be this unity and to remain this unity!

Eckhart addresses himself to the second part of the Epistle of James that he read for the day. It is a lesson of *doing* the word and not merely taking it in, of working to make the seed grow.

Accept and submit to the word which has been planted in you and can save your souls. But you must do what the word tells you, and not just listen to it and deceive yourselves. To listen to the word and not obey is like looking at your own features in a mirror and then, after a quick look, going off and immediately forgetting what you looked like.

Nobody must imagine that he is religious while he still goes on deceiving himself and not keeping control over his tongue; anyone who does this has the wrong idea of religion. Pure, unspoilt religion, in the eyes of God our Father is this: coming to the help of orphans and widows when they need it, and keeping oneself uncontaminated by the world. (Jm. 1:21–24,26,27)

James urges us to summon all our discipline in order to "listen to the word and obey it" and to "actively put it into practice." The artistic calling is a demanding one.

Eckhart invokes here the two commandments —love of God and of neighbor—that Jesus exhorts us to (Mk. 12:31; 22:39) and points out that what James is telling us we ought to have learned from our journey inward: *that love is all-encompassing.* To love oneself *is* to love one's neighbor if we love ourselves correctly. For we are all one with each other in the sea of God. *We should love them*

just as much as ourselves, and that is not difficult.
True love, for the person who has made the spiritual journey that Eckhart has outlined in three paths, is not a moral imperative. It is *more of a reward than a command,* because it is *something we long for.* It is a *pleasure* to do the acts of love out of a flow and an artistry and a creativity and an overflow that is the basis of all true art. For to love God is to love those in God and to celebrate with them. It is like living in *the kingdom of heaven* to be able to *rejoice in their joys as much as in our own joy* and to *long for their honor as much as for our own honor.* For the kingdom of heaven consists of such a celebrative banquet of blessings shared. All those who are blessed with birthing possibilities come to this banquet to celebrate. "Wait only for this birth within yourself, and you will discover all blessing and all consolation, all bliss, all being, and all truth. If you neglect this, you will neglect all blessing and all happiness." We create from this blessedness: "In this same ground all of God's friends will receive their blessedness and create from it. That is the 'table in the kingdom of God.'" At this table the gifts of the Spirit flow like a rapid river and we do not become obstacles

to such flowing, but ourselves drink of it and pass on its ever-flowing energies.

This is the word that has been "planted in us and can save our souls," as James puts it—the word of our own creativity and rebirth as sons of the Creator and heirs of divine creativity. Because our salvation lies in our making contact with our divine origins, and it pertains to divinity to create, therefore our salvation lies in creativity. For in the work of the artist, subject/object distinctions are broken through and we experience the unity of all creation once again, the unity of the circle of being that resides in the Godhead. Healing now takes place. And this healing is salvation, a unity in what Schürmann calls an "operative identity." It is a healing between us and the Creator and between us and creation and between our deepest inner self and our outgoing self. From all these unions a saving child is born. And its name is Beauty or the glory *(doxa)* of the children of creation. The work of the artist is to carve out and unveil the glory that is hidden in creation.

If a skilled artist makes an image of wood or stone, he or she does not place that image within the wood but chisels away the pieces that have hidden and covered it up. The artist contributes nothing to the wood but rather takes away and removes the covering and takes away the blight; then what lay hidden underneath shines forth. This is the treasure that lay hidden in the soil, as our Lord says in the Gospel. (Mt. 13:44)

This unveiling of a shining treasure brings about healing and salvation. "This, then, is salvation, when we marvel at the beauty of created things and praise the beautiful providence of their Creator or when we purchase heavenly goods by our compassion for the works of creation."

THE VIA TRANSFORMATIVA

In the Via Transformativa, Divinity is experienced as compassion, that is, as healing and justice-making and as celebration. Eckhart says, "What happens to another, be that a joy or a sorrow, happens to me." This is the essence of compassion: interdependence. We are already inside one another. Today's physics is rediscovering this ancient mystical truth, that every being in the universe is sharing atoms from every other being and that all beings are, as Eckhart says, "interdependent." Here lies the basis for compassionate living.

In compassion we become like God because God is "the compassionate one" in the Jewish tradition. "Compassion divinely adorns the soul, clothing it in the robe which is proper to God," Eckhart says. Compassion is about doing or acting out of our shared interdependence and this is what the prophet Isaiah celebrates when he asks:

Is this not the sort of fast that please me
—it is the Lord Yahweh who speaks—
to break unjust fetters
and undo the thongs of the yoke,

to let the oppressed go free,
and break every yoke,
to share your bread with the hungry,
and shelter the homeless poor?   (Is. 58:6,7)

And is this not the teaching of the Cosmic Christ as the Christ who is present in all who suffer? Jesus taught as much when he said, "I tell you solemnly, insofar as you did this to one of the least of these brothers or sisters of mine, you did it to me" (Mt. 25:40). It is in compassion that we imitate God and this is why Jesus says in his Sermon on the Mount in Luke's gospel: "Be you compassionate as your Creator in heaven is compassionate" (Lk. 6:36). He is calling us to our divine work in the world.

Compassion is a kind of passion, a passion for justice and healing and celebration. But it is more than that. It also requires our intelligence and our clear-headed capacity for weighing options and making sound decisions. Eckhart says:

We therefore are compassionate like the Father when we are compassionate not from passion, not from impulse, but from deliberate choice and reasonable decision. For Psalm 84 says: "Compassion and truth meet one another," that is, passion and reason.

In compassion, as the psalmist says, "justice and peace have kissed" (Ps. 85:10). Prophecy and mysticism come together in compassion, making it the culmination of the spiritual journey. The previous three paths find their deepest expression in compassion.

COMPASSION IS
AN OCEAN – THE MYSTICAL
SIDE TO COMPASSION

*"Have compassion on the people
who are in you."* (Ho. 14:4)

The prophet says: "Lord, have compassion on
the people who are in you" (Ho. 14:4). Our Lord
answered: "All who are sick I will heal, and I will
love them freely."

I will take for my text the words "The Pharisee
asked the Lord to eat with him" and, further,
"Our Lord said to the woman: *Vade in pace,* go in
peace!" (Lk. 7:36,50). It is good when someone
goes from peace to peace. It is praiseworthy. However, it is not enough. One should *run* into peace,
one should not begin in peace. God, our Lord,
means: One should be grounded in peace and
thrown into peace and should end up in peace.
Our Lord says: "In me alone shall be your peace"

(Jn. 16:33). Just so far as we are in God we are in peace. If any part of us is in God, it has peace; if any part of us is outside of God it has no peace. Saint John says: "Everything that is born of God overcomes the world" (1 Jn. 5:4). What is born of God seeks peace and runs into peace. Therefore he said: *"Vade in pace,* run into peace." The person who runs and runs, continually running into peace, is a heavenly person. The heavens are continually running and in their running they seek peace.

Now pay attention! "The Pharisee asked our Lord to eat with him." The food which I eat is united to my body as my body is united to my soul. My body and my soul are united in one being but not in one activity—as my soul is united in one work with the eye, that is to see; thus the food I eat is united in one being with my nature but not in one activity, and this signifies the great union that we will have with God in being but not in activity. Therefore the Pharisee asked our Lord to eat with him.

The word "Pharisee" means one who is set apart and does not know of any end. Everything belonging to the soul should be completely stripped off. The nobler the powers are, the more they strip off. Some powers are so high above the body and so detached that they peel away and separate off completely! A master says a beautiful word: "What has once touched corporal things never enters again." The second meaning of Pharisee is that one should be stripped off and detached and gathered inward. From this one can conclude that an unlearned person can learn knowledge and teach others through love and desire. The third meaning of Pharisee is that one should have no end and should not be closed off and should cling to nothing and should be so fully grounded in peace that he or she knows nothing more of strife, when such a person is grounded in God through the powers that are entirely stripped off. Therefore the prophet said: "Lord, have compassion on the people who are in you."

A master says: "The highest work that God has ever worked in all creatures is compassion." The most secret and forbidden work that he ever worked on the angels was carrying them up into compassion; this is the work of compassion as it is in itself and as it is in God. Whatever God does, the first outburst is always compassion, and I do not mean that he forgives a person his sins or that a person takes compassion on another. The master means much more. He means that the *highest* work that God works is compassion. A master says: "The work of compassion is so close to God that although truth and riches and goodness name God, one of them names him better than the other." The highest work of God is compassion and this means that God sets the soul in the highest and purest place which it can occupy: in space, in the sea, in a fathomless ocean; and there God works compassion. Therefore the prophet says: "Lord, have compassion on the people who are in you."

What people are in God? Saint John says: "God is love and whoever remains in love remains in God and God in him" (1 Jn. 4:16). Although Saint John says that love unites, love never establishes anything in God. Perhaps it connects something that is already united to him. Love does not unite, not in any way. What is already united it sticks together and binds. Love unites in works but not in being. The best masters say that reason peels entirely away and takes God unveiled, as he is, pure Being in himself. Knowledge breaks through truth and goodness and falls on pure Being and takes God naked, as he is without name. But I say: neither knowledge nor love unites. Love apprehends God himself insofar as he is good, and if God lost the name "Goodness" that would be the end of love. Love takes God under a skin, under a cloak. Reason does not do this. It takes God insofar as God is known to it. Reason can never comprehend him in the ocean of his unfathomableness. I say that beyond these two, beyond knowledge and love, there is compassion. In the highest and purest acts that God works, God works compassion.

A master says these beautiful words: "There is in the soul something very secret and hidden and far above it, from which the powers of reason and will break forth." Saint Augustine says: "Where the Son breaks out from the Father in the first outpouring is ineffable; so too there is something very secret about the first outbreak, where reason and the will break forth." A master who has spoken the best about the soul says that all human science can never fathom what the soul is in its ground. To know what the soul is, one needs supernatural knowledge. We do not know about what the powers of the soul do when they go out to do their work; we know a little about this, but not very much. What the soul is in its ground, no one knows. What one can know about it must be supernatural, it must be from grace. The soul is where God works compassion. Amen.

COMMENTARY

WHAT IS SOUL? / THE FULLEST OF ALL GOD'S
WORKS IS COMPASSION / COMPASSION IS AN
UNFATHOMABLE OCEAN GREATER THAN
KNOWLEDGE AND LOVE / WE ARE IN
COMPASSION WHEN WE ARE IN GOD / HOW
THIS INNESS OF PANENTHEISM DESTROYS ALL
OTHERNESS AND CREATES INTERDEPENDENCE /
THE NEED TO RUN INTO PEACE

Notice the startling way in which Eckhart ends
this sermon. He is groping for a definition of
soul, saying that the soul is so deep and mysteri-
ous that we can never know it—only supernatural
knowledge will reveal it to us. *What the soul is in its
ground no one knows.* But then he startles all of us,
himself included no doubt, when he says simply:
The soul is where God works compassion. Amen. In
other words, if compassion does not work
through us, we do not have soul yet. Soul is our
capacity for compassion, divine compassion. Soul
is something we acquire; it is our capacity for
compassion.

In the present sermon, Eckhart examines the mystical side to compassion, the side of consciousness itself. For Eckhart, compassion is not merely a moral norm. It is a consciousness, a way of seeing the world and responding to the world. It is a way of living out the truth of our inness with God and with one another as discovered in Path One. Compassion presumes a certain mystical consciousness or way of seeing the world. What is that way?

Eckhart repeats his conviction that God is compassion. His sermon is based on the prophet Hosea, who, in Eckhart's translation of the Bible, said: *"Lord, have compassion on the people who are in you"* (Ho. 14:4), and who in a current translation says: "You are the one in whom orphans find compassion." In both translations the word *in* plays a prominent role and Eckhart, as we shall see shortly, develops his theology of compassion from his theology of inness or panentheism. But Eckhart says more about compassion and God in this sermon. Following Peter Lombard and Thomas Aquinas, Eckhart declares that *compassion is the highest work that God has ever worked in all creatures.* Compassion, Eckhart says, is the origin of all God's creativity—God's motivation and

God's goal. *Whatever God does, the first outburst is always compassion.* Compassion is *the highest work that God works.* Compassion is fuller and deeper than either love or knowledge. *Beyond these two, beyond knowledge and love, there is compassion.* Compassion is the best name there is for God. It alone comes close to naming the creative works of God, for *in the highest and purest acts that God works, God works compassion.* Compassion is therefore the one blessing and the one fruit that remains from creation through resurrection. It is the origin of all God's creativity and the fullness of all fruitful birthing. "For it is indeed a blessing when something bears fruit and the fruit remains. The fruit, however, remains to the one who remains there in love." If we are to imitate God and to bear the fruit that God bears and to bear the Son of God and indeed to become the Son of God, then compassion is the ultimate way of our spiritual journeying. Where does this God-like way take us?

It takes us into God. The breakthrough that gave birth to the Son and the breakthrough that gives us a second birth both come from the same ground. We cannot name the ground for we cannot put our fingers on it—*what the soul is in its ground, no one knows.* It takes supernatural grace

even to enter there. However, we can name the
energy that goes on there, the fire that is burning
by the blaze of the *scintilla animae* in the core of
the soul. What goes on there is compassion—*that
is where God works compassion*. In our very inner
core, as innermost as we can get and as innermost
as we are, God is busy working compassion. Eckhart hints that just as the best name for the
unnameable God is Compassion, so too the finest
name for the unnameable soul is Compassion. After all, the innermost part of the soul *is* the *imago
Dei*. Where we create from our innermost being
we are always creating compassion. In the text
that Eckhart used for this sermon, Hosea an-
nounces:

> Let the wise man understand these words.
> Let the intelligent man grasp their meaning.
> For the ways of Yahweh are straight,
> and virtuous men walk in them,
> but sinners stumble.   (Ho. 14:9–10)

All our fruitfulness comes from God who is the
Compassionate one. Thus Compassion is the
source of all creativity and birthing. And of all the
fruits we give birth to, none is more Godly than
the way of walking that is Yahweh's way, a way of
walking in compassion.

Not only is compassion in us at our very core, where God energizes us and divinizes us into creators ourselves, but we are in compassion. For, as we learned in Path One, God is not only in us but we are in God. If God is Compassion, then our journeying into compassion is necessarily our journeying into God and vice versa. The deeper we go into God, the deeper we go into compassion.

Eckhart gropes, searching and stretching his own imagination, for images of the panentheistic existence of being in God and in compassion that he finds in John's Gospel and in the prophet Hosea. Eckhart calls compassion an ocean. Compassion is not only an ocean, it is a *fathomless ocean*, it is not only a sea, it is *space* itself. Eckhart is driven into cosmic language and driven to call on his cosmic experience in an effort to picture compassion. A compassionate consciousness presumes a cosmic consciousness.

> Compassion means that God sets the soul in the highest and purest place which it can occupy: in space, in the sea, in a fathomless ocean; and there God works compassion. Therefore the prophet says: "Lord, have compassion on the people who are in you."

This picture of God setting the soul in an ocean of compassion conjures up images of swimming and floating—yes, even skinny-dipping—in compassion. We are suspended, Eckhart is saying, in a sea of divine grace called compassion. We breathe compassion in and breathe compassion out daily if we are awake and aware. He turns to John's imagery of our panentheistic swimming in compassion:

> Anyone who lives in love lives in God,
> and God lives in him.
> Love will come to its perfection in us
> when we can face the day of Judgment without
>   fear;
> because even in this world
> we have become as he is.   (1 Jn. 4:16–17)

Clearly, for Eckhart, a consciousness of our inness in God is a consciousness of our inness in compassion. If Compassion is God's name and we have become as he is, then we have become compassion. A son or daughter of God is a son or daughter of compassion.

This sermon is an immensely maternal one. Eckhart's images of the divine sea of compassion conjure up images of the divine, maternal womb. Eckhart is saying that we are born in a sea of compassion, a compassionate fluid of divinely maternal grace. In painting these images Eckhart recalls the biblical roots for the word compassion. In Hebrew the word for compassion and the word for womb come from the same stem, *rehem* and *rahamim*. Compassion is a return to our origin.

What are some consequences of this breakthrough in consciousness by which we are awakened to the fact of our swimming in a space and a sea of compassion? One consequence is the breakdown of all dualistic thinking. For we are not alone in this divine sea. All creatures have been born in the same holy fluid; we do not swim alone but in a common sea of oneness with others. This means that all beings are interdependent. "God's peace prompts fraternal service, so that one creature sustains the other. One is enriching the other, that is why *all creatures are interdependent.*" Creatures in this common sea serve one another and sustain one another. Eckhart's consciousness of interdependence is crucial to grasping what true compassion is about. Indeed, the late Thomas Merton defined compassion as a "keen awareness of the interdependence of all living beings which are all part of one another and all involved in one another."

Another consequence of our swimming to-

in one act of love. Eckhart says: "He who loves God more than his neighbor loves him well, it is true, but not perfectly." Why not? Ancelet comments:

Eckhart takes literally and in all its rigor the Gospel precept: to love God is "the first and greatest commandment," but the second, to love one's neighbor as oneself is "quite like" unto it. He understands by this that for him who loves his neighbor as he should be loved, that is to say, in God, there can only be one sole love.

Our love of self is the same way. When we are *grounded in God* we become *so fully grounded in peace that we know nothing more of strife.* When we are truly in God and in compassion we are *grounded in peace and thrown into peace and end up in peace.*

But Eckhart makes an important point: we ought not to exaggerate the experience of our inness with God and compassion to the detriment of our need to develop compassion and to seek it out in our work and activities. Indeed, we need to *run into peace.* We are not yet fully there, even though compassion is the starting point of our creation and the goal of it. It is *not enough to go from peace to peace* or to narcissistically meditate on our compassionate origins. We need to seek peace, to make peace, to *run into peace. What is born of God seeks peace and runs into peace.* Like the vast stars in the heavens, we must be on the move in this cosmic space that is peace. Indeed, a heavenly person will imitate the cosmos itself and will always be on the move toward peace. Such a person is a verb, not a noun, *running and running continually into peace.* Compassion too will be a verb and not a noun. After all, God's work is continually in process. God is always giving birth and desiring to give birth and his birth is always from compassion and toward compassion. Our work needs to be the same. Our union with God as Compassion is a union of being but not yet a union of activity. Compassion as being, then, has already begun. But compassion as work needs to be done. One activity of compassion is that of forgiving others, as Jesus does in Luke's Gospel (7:36–50). But that activity too must derive its full energy from the inness behind compassion before it is truly a compassionate work. For outside the sea of compassion, there is no compassion. Outside God there is nothing but nothing. But inside God there are all things so bathed in compassion that we can say with John: *"Everything that is born of God overcomes the world."* Compassion, which had the first word, will eventually have the last.

SERMON

JUSTICE, THE WORK OF COMPASSION

*"The just will live forever and their reward
is with the Lord."* (Ws. 5:16)

These words are in the Epistle for today and are
spoken by the wise person: "The just shall live
forever" (Ws. 5:16). From time to time I have said
what a just person is, but now I say it with a different meaning: A just person is one who is
conformed and transformed into justice. The just
person lives in God and God in her or him. Thus
God will be born in this just person and the just
person is born into God; and therefore God will
be born through every virtue of the just person
and will rejoice through every virtue of the just
person. And not only at every virtue will God
rejoice but especially at every *work* of the just person, however small it is. When this work is done
through justice and results in justice, God will

rejoice at it, indeed, God will rejoice through and through; for nothing remains in his ground which does not tickle God through and through out of joy. Ignorant people have to believe this, but enlightened ones should know it.

The just person does not seek anything with his work, for every single person who seeks anything or even something with his or her works is working for a why and is a servant and a mercenary. Therefore, if you wish to be conformed and transformed into justice, do not intend anything in your work and strive for no why, either in time or in eternity. Do not aim at reward or blessedness, neither this nor that. For such works are truly fully dead. Indeed, I say that even if you take God as your goal, all such works which you do with this intention are dead and you will spoil good works. And not only will you spoil good works but you will also sin, for you will be like a gardener who was supposed to plant a garden but instead uprooted the trees and then wanted to have a reward for it. In this way you will spoil good works. Therefore, if you want to live and if you want your works to live, you must be dead to all things and you must become in touch with nothingness. It is peculiar to the creature that it makes something from something; but it is peculiar to God to make something from nothing. Therefore, for God to make something in you or with you, you must first make contact with this nothingness. Therefore, enter into your own ground and work there and these works which you work there will all be living. And therefore the wise person says: "The just person lives." For because he is just, he works and his works live.

Now the wise person says: "His reward is with the Lord." Now take a minute to consider this. If he says "with," that means that the reward of the just person is there where God himself is; for the blessedness of the just person and the blessedness of God are *one* blessedness, because the just person is blessed where God is blessed. Saint John says this: "The Word was with God" (Jn. 1:1). He also says "with," and therefore the just person is like God, since God is justice. And therefore whoever is in justice is in God and is God.

Now we will speak further about the word "just." The Book of Wisdom does not say "the just person" or "the just angel" but, rather, only "the just." The Father gives birth to his Son as the Just One and the Just One as his Son; for all virtue of the just and every work of the just which

are born from the virtue of the just person are
nothing other than the event of the Son being
born from the Father. Therefore the Father never
rests; he always runs and hurries in order that the
Son be born in me, as the Scriptures say: "For
Zion's sake I will not hold my peace and for Jerusalem's sake I will not rest, until the just are
revealed and shine forth like a flash of lightning"
(Is. 62:1). "Zion" means the fullness of life and
"Jerusalem" means the fullness of peace. Indeed,
God rests neither for the fullness of life nor for
the fullness of peace; he always runs and hurries
for this purpose, that the just person may be
made known. In the just nothing should work except God alone. For all works are surely dead if
anything from the outside compels you to work.
Even if God were to compel you to work from the
outside, then such works would surely all be dead.
If your works are to live, then God must move you
inwardly, in the innermost part of the soul, if they
are really to live. There is your life and there
alone you live.

And I say that if one virtue seems greater than
another and if you hold it in greater esteem than
the other, then you do not live it as it is in justice
and God does not work in you. For as long as a

person values or loves one virtue more than another, he does not love and take the virtues as
they are in justice; nor is such a person just. For
the just person loves and works all virtues in justice as they are justice itself. Scripture says:
"Before the creation of the world, I am"
(Si. 24:9). This means "Before I am" which
means that if a person is raised up beyond time
into eternity, then the person works one work
there with God. Some people ask how a person
can work these works which God has worked a
thousand years ago and which God will work a
thousand years from now and they do not understand it. In eternity there is no before and no
after. Therefore, what happened a thousand years
ago and what will happen a thousand years from
now and what is now happening is one in eternity.
Therefore, what God did a thousand years ago
and has done and what he will do in a thousand
years and what he is now doing—all this is nothing but one work. Therefore a person who is risen
beyond time into eternity works with God what
God worked a thousand years ago and will work a
thousand years hence. This too is for wise people
a matter of knowledge and for ignorant people a
matter for belief.

Saint Paul says: "We are eternally chosen in the Son" (Ep. 1:4). Therefore we should never rest until we become what we have eternally been in him (Rm. 8:29ff.). For the Father runs and hurries in order that we be born in the Son and become the same as what the Son is. The Father begets his Son and in this birthing the Father takes so great a rest and a pleasure that his entire nature is absorbed in it. For whatever is always in God moves him to beget; indeed, from his ground, from his essence, and from his being the Father is moved to beget.

Sometimes there is revealed in the soul a light and a person thinks he is the Son and yet it is only a light. For when the Son is revealed in the soul, the love of the Holy Spirit is also revealed there. Therefore I say that it is the essence of the Father to beget the Son and the essence of the Son that I be born in him and in his image. It is the essence of the Holy Spirit that I should be burned into him and should be completely consumed in him and become entirely love. Whoever is in love and, in this way, has become entirely love thinks that God loves no one but himself alone. And he knows of no one else who has loved anything else or has been loved by anyone else except by God alone.

Some professors maintain that the spirit receives its blessedness from love; others maintain that it receives it from the contemplation of God. But I say: It receives it neither from love nor from knowledge nor from contemplation. Now one might ask: Has the spirit no vision of God in eternal life? Yes and no. Insofar as it is born, it has no contemplation and no vision more of God. But insofar as it is being born, it has a vision of God. Therefore the blessedness of the spirit lies where it is born and not where it has been born, for it lives where the Father lives. This means in the simplicity and the nakedness of being. Therefore turn away from all things and take yourself naked into being. For what is outside of being is an accident and all accidents bring about a why.

That we "live forever," may God help us. Amen.

COMMENTARY

GOD IS JUSTICE AND TO BE IN GOD IS TO BE IN
JUSTICE / BIRTH AND BREAKTHROUGH ARE
RESURRECTIONS INTO JUSTICE / TOWARD A
SPIRITUALITY OF WORK: WORKING WITHOUT A
WHY OR WHEREFORE / OUR WORK, GIVING
BIRTH TO THE NEW CREATION

Eckhart has an entire theology of work and it is based on his theology of creativity, justice, and compassion. We saw this theology of work as art and creativity in the Via Creativa. In the present sermon Eckhart explores the subject of work from the perspective of justice. Only work for justice and out of justice is *living work*. This kind of work makes God delighted—*God rejoices . . . especially at every work of the just person, however small it is*. Why is this? Because *God is justice*. Elsewhere Eckhart says that "God is the most just—*justissimus.*" Again, "God is, as it were, justice itself." Therefore to be in God is to be both in compassion and in justice. Indeed, "compassion means justice." Because "God and justice are completely

one," Eckhart can say in the present sermon that
whoever is in justice is in God and is God. So con-
vinced is Eckhart that to be in justice is to be in
God and to be in God is to be in justice that he
can say elsewhere: "If God were not just, the just
person could not consider God." And again,
"Since God is justice you must embrace justice as
it is in itself, as it is in God."

We are called to do justice in all our work, but
first we need to be reborn into justice. For our
true breakthrough and birth is a resurrection
into justice and into God who is Justice. The birth
of the divine Word is a birth of Justice. "For the
just person, the 'word' of justice is justice itself, as
we read later in the tenth chapter of John: 'I and
the Father are one.' For the just person denotes
justice alone." Our birth is to be a *conformation
and transformation into justice.* After all, if the Word
of God by nature is the "Son of Justice," then we
who are the adopted words—the bywords—and
adopted sons of God must also be sons and
daughters of justice.

> The just person is the "word" of justice, by means
> of which justice declares and manifests itself . . .
> The just person is the offspring and son of justice.
> He is called, and actually is, the son because he

> becomes different in person but not in nature . . .
> Now if the Father and the Son, justice and the just
> man, are one and the same in nature, it follows that
> the just man is equal to, not less than, justice.

Since justice, like compassion, lies at the very core
of the Godhead and at the center of the origin of
our existence, our being born is a being born out
of justice. "The just person is always in the process of being born from justice itself, just as he has
been born from it from the beginning, ever since
he has been just." If the just person is the "word"
of justice and if a word is that which flows out but
remains within as we saw in Path One, then the
just person is rooted in justice at the same time
that such a person is birthing justice. Eckhart
links the birth into justice with the moment of
breakthrough and of resurrection when he discusses the new experience of time—*in eternity there
is no before and no after.* We are told to *rise beyond
time,* to be resurrected from a time consciousness
that thinks in terms of before and after, since that
is the kind of time framework in which our own
birthing takes place. To substantiate this point,
Eckhart draws on wisdom literature and on Paul.
In the Book of Ecclesiasticus we read:

> From eternity, in the beginning, he created me,
>   and for eternity I shall remain . . .
> I am like a vine putting out graceful shoots,
>   my blossoms bear the fruit of glory and
>   wealth . . .
> Approach me, you who desire me,
>   and take your fill of my fruits,
> for memories of me are sweeter than honey,
>   inheriting me is sweeter than the
>   honeycomb.   (Si. 24:9,17,19–20)

And from Paul—not from Plato—there is a hint of this same preexistence in a time before time, a time beyond time:

> Blessed be God the Father of our Lord Jesus
>   Christ,
> who has blessed us with all the spiritual
>   blessings of heaven in Christ.
> Before the world was made, he chose us, chose
>   us in Christ,
> to be holy and spotless, and to live through love
>   in his presence,
> determining that we should become his
>   adopted sons, through Jesus Christ . . .
>   (Ep. 1:3–5)

And so, in Eckhart's as in Paul's theology, our rebirth as sons of God took place "before the world was made," that is to say in eternity. This link between our rebirth and the preexistence of

Wisdom is made again in Romans, where Paul writes:

> They are the ones he chose specially long ago and intended to become true images of his Son, so that his Son might be the eldest of many brothers. (Rm. 8:29)

Eckhart cautions that some people have already tasted of this eternity he speaks of—they *know* what he is talking about; others have still to believe in it. The *enlightened ones know*; the *ignorant believe* in these matters. It is evident that another scriptural text that Eckhart had in front of him for this sermon is from the prophet Isaiah, chapter 62. In that chapter the author discusses themes that have inspired Eckhart's treatise on justice and God—themes of the integrity of virtue that the just person maintains; themes of God's silence and of God's *running* and *hurrying* and of God's joy.

> About Zion I will not be silent,
> about Jerusalem I will not grow weary,
> until her integrity shines out like the dawn
> and her salvation flames like a torch.
>
> The nations then will see your integrity,
> all the kings your glory,
> and you will be called by a new name . . .
> but you shall be called "My Delight" . . .

> You who keep Yahweh mindful
> must take no rest.
> Nor let him take rest
> till he has restored Jerusalem,
> and made her
> the boast of the earth.   (Is. 62:1-2,4,6-7)

Eckhart recognizes the similarity between Isaiah 62 and Wisdom 5 where both traditions, that of the prophets and that of wisdom literature, appeal to the royal throne as a symbol for justice. Isaiah says:

> You are to be a crown of splendor in the hand
>   of Yahweh,
> a princely diadem in the hand of your God.
>   (Is. 62:3)

Wisdom speaks:

> But the virtuous live for ever,
> their recompense lies with the Lord,
> the Most High takes care of them.
> So they shall receive the royal crown of
>   splendor,
> the diadem of beauty from the hand of the
>   Lord;
> for he will shelter them with his right hand
> and shield them with his arm . . .
>
> he will put on justice as a breastplate.
>   (Ws. 5:15-17,18)

The theme of a royal birth is very much in accord with Eckhart's treatment of our birth as the birth

of a Godly Word, the birth of Justice. The fruit we
are to bear is to be "neither more nor less than
God himself," that would mean neither more nor
less than Justice. When God's he becomes I, then
"God and the soul are eternally doing one work
very fruitfully." This fruitful work is also a blessing. Eckhart's theology of blessing reaches a
crescendo in the works of justice and compassion.
The *blessedness of the just person and the blessedness of*
God is one blessedness because the just person is blessed
where God is blessed. Justice is a name for the full
blessing of God.

Here, then, lies the basis for Eckhart's theology of work: he envisions a trinity of word, birth,
work. Our true work is from the creative Word
itself. Eckhart's theology of work is based on his
theology of the Word that flows out but remains
within. You cannot separate word from work in
Eckhart's thinking, for the truthful word is always
fruitful and leads to the authentic work. They are
related as fruit and vine. Indeed, the Word is the
work when work is authentic. What is authentic
work? Work that is without a why. Works that have
an outside purpose to them are *truly fully dead.*
Even if God is inserted as an outside purpose,
such a work is spoiled. True work is ecstasy—an

end in itself. It is the ecstasy that justice brings
and the ecstasy that the work itself brings to self,
others, or God. *The just person does not seek anything
with his work; for every single person who seeks anything
or even something with their works is working for a why
and is a servant and a mercenary.* It is part of the
merchant mentality to allow alienation and separation to come between us and our work. To work
without a why is to touch one's origin. "The end
is universally the same as the beginning. It has no
'why' or 'wherefore' but is itself the 'why' of and
for all things: 'I am the beginning and the end' "
(Rv. 1:8). In this return to our origin we are also
returning to the marriage of work and Word, for
the Word is what "was in the beginning." When
our work is without a why, it is a work of love, for
love

> has no why. If I had a friend and loved him because
> good and all I wished came to me through him, I
> wouldn't love my friend but myself. I ought to love
> my friend for his own goodness and for his own
> virtue and for everything that he is in himself.

Just as we are to love without a why and be just
without a why, so are we to work without a why.
Such work is a work of love, for "whoever is born

of God as a son of God loves God for his sake, that
is to say, he loves God for the sake of loving God
and does all his work for the sake of working."
Our works that are done in God are to be works of
justice.

> Where justice is at work, you are at work, because
> you could not but do the works of justice. Yes, even
> if hell were to interfere with the course of justice,
> you still would do the works of justice, and hell
> itself would not constitute any suffering; hell would
> be joy because you yourself would be justice, and
> that is why you could not but do the works of jus-
> tice.

Elsewhere Eckhart defines justice as "a certain
rightness whereby every person receives his or
her due." We *do* the work of justice when we bring
about this "certain rightness" among persons. Indeed, it is our just works that make us live. "For
the just person as such to act justly is to live; indeed, justice is his life, his being alive, his being,
insofar as he is just." Like life itself, justice is its
own reward. "The just person lives and works
without reason of gain. As much as life has the
reason for living in itself, in that same way the just
person knows no other reason for being just."

Justice is the reason for justice. Just work is the reason for work.

To work without a why is to work from one's inner self. Therefore Eckhart advises the person interested in good work to *enter into your own ground and work there, and these works which you work there will all be living.* Living works come from where life is: from our inner core where no why or wherefore enters, where all is one.

> God's ground is my ground and my ground is God's ground. Here I live on my own as God lives on her own . . . You should work all your works out of this innermost ground without why. Indeed, I say, so long as you work for the kingdom of heaven, or for God, or for your internal happiness and thus for something outward, all is not well with you.

Outside motivation is not worthy of the work we do. It separates us from our work and alienates us from our inner self. That way lies spiritual and personal death. When we work in that fashion our work is dead work.

> Those deeds which do not flow from within your inner self are all dead before God. Those are the deeds which were engendered by causes outside of yourself, because they did not proceed from life.

That is why they are dead, because only that is alive which has motion within itself. Consequently, for a person's deeds to be alive, they have to come from within, not from something alien and outside himself or herself.

One reason why outside-oriented works alienate us is that they are born of compulsion and not compassion or creativity, the way the creative Word gives birth. *All works are surely dead if anything from the outside compels you to work. Even if God* did the compelling, they would be dead. Psychologist William Eckhardt makes a similar observation when he insists that compulsion is the Number One psychological obstacle to compassion and works of compassion. Meister Eckhart urges us to void all compulsion in our work. We should "become accustomed to work without compulsion," he insists. How do we do this? By working from within, from our own being and needs of being, and not from outside. Many people are "being worked rather than working." Such persons should learn to "cooperate with" God. This is learned from making contact with one's inner person. It is from inside, as Jesus taught, that works are made holy.

People never need to think so much about what they ought to do, but they should remember what they are. Now if people and their ways are good, their works might shine forth brightly. If you are just, then your works are also just. One does not think of basing holiness on one action, one should base holiness on being. For works do not sanctify us, but we should sanctify the works . . . One should apply oneself with all diligence to being good, not so much to what one should do, of what nature the works are, but of what nature the ground of the works is.

When we are truly grounded, it is God who is involved in our works.

Such a person carries God in all his works and at all places, and all this person's works are done purely by God, for if anyone is the cause of the work it is more properly and really God's than that of the person who performs the work. If then we fix our minds on God purely and simply, then indeed God must perform our works and no one can hinder God in all her works, neither multitude nor place.

Such work is an occasion for expression and even reception of our divinity since it is a share in God's work. We return God's creative work—her compassion—to her.

The person whose aims and affections are thus fixed on God in all his works, to him God gives her divinity. All that this person works God works, for my humility gives God her divinity . . . God is not only the beginning of all our works and of our being, but also the end and rest of all beings.

God is the beginning of our work of compassion and justice because God is "in the beginning," and when we are in God who is Compassion and Justice, and so firmly grounded there that our actions flow from this source, then God too flows from this source. The new creation is God's too—though we are the instruments for it. God is eager to flow into our work—"God wants to do your work herself," and will, "if you will only follow and resist her not at all." One might even say that God depends on us for the divine work of compassion and justice to happen: "Just as little as I can do anything without God, she cannot really accomplish anything apart from me."

What makes works live and makes them just and compassionate is the fact that they come from deep within. *If your works are to live, then God must move you inwardly, in the innermost part of the soul, if they are really to live. There is your life and there alone you live.* Only this kind of work is pleasing to

God and returns a blessing to God. "There, in the
soul's innermost part, God works; there all works
please God. No work will ever be acceptable to
God unless it is accomplished there." There is no
conflict, no dualism between the "outside world"
and the innermost self, for the innermost self,
filled with a consciousness of interdependence
and panentheism, is itself capable of unifying outside and inside. Here lies the cure for
compulsion.

> One should not escape from the inward person, or
> flee from him or deny him, but in him, with him,
> and through him, one should learn to act in such a
> way that one breaks up the inwardness into reality
> and leads reality into inwardness, and that one
> should thus become accustomed to work without
> compulsion.

The so-called outside world also is divine.

> You might say: "A person must turn outward if he
> or she has to do external things, for no work can be
> done except in its own form." That is quite true,
> but the external form of images is nothing external
> for experienced people, since all things have for an
> inward person an inward divine mode of being.

Art as meditation, then, is not from the outside
but from deep within, for even external forms of

images come from that source in the experienced person. Work is not less divine because it is busy with external things; it is less divine if it does not flow from the innermost divine sources. It is from the inside that work is made vast and Godly.

> The inward work is God-like and Godly, and it suggests the divine attributes in this respect: this outward work, its quality and its size, its length and its breadth, does not in the least increase the goodness of the inward work; it has its goodness in itself.

This is why all vocations are holy, all work is divine and is a divine vocation. "You should know and you should have considered to what vocation you are most strongly called by God. For all people are not called to God in one way, as Saint Paul says" in 1 Corinthians 12:4–11. If the work is from inside, from our inness with God who is Justice and Compassion, it is God's work and of divine size.

> The outward work can never be small if the inward one is great, and the outward can never be great or good if the inward is small or of little worth. The inward work always includes in itself all size, all breadth and length. The inward work receives and draws all its being from nowhere else but from and in the heart of God.

Drawing its energy from the divine energy, all work that proceeds from the inside of oneself and from the "heart of God" is abundant and divine. It is also free, like God's creative Word and work are free. God is free and untrammeled in all the divine works, and she works them out of genuine love. *That* person who is united with God does exactly the same thing. He or she also is free and untrammeled in all his or her works and works them solely for God's honor and does not seek his or her own; and God acts in that person.

There is still another dimension—and a divine dimension it is—to our work when it is grounded from the inside of ourselves. In our acts of creation we are imitating the ground of all creation, the Creator or Father of all being and all works. But this Father is always giving birth. *From his ground, from his essence, and from his being the Father is moved to beget.* Indeed, it is the very *essence of the Father* to birth the Son. *It is the essence of the Father to beget the Son.* If this be the case, then, where my ground becomes the Father's ground, we give birth together and the Son is born at the time that the new creation is birthed. And the Father is eager and even busy to see this happen. Our work —so long as it originates in our center and inner core—is the birthing of God's Son, the Cosmic Christ. The new creation is even more splendid than the first creation. "Always bear in mind that the faithful and loving God brought humankind out of a sinful life into a divine life. He made out of his enemy a friend, which is more than to create a new world." In the new creation *we work one work there with God.* There, in the bosom of Justice itself, all history is born anew. The Father gives birth to his *Son as the Just One and the Just One as his Son; for all virtue of the just and every work of the just . . . are nothing other than the event of the Son being born from the Father.* Thus our work becomes the Son, the new creation, the fruit of the "whole creation eagerly waiting for God to reveal his sons," a creation that "has been groaning in one great act of giving birth" (Rm. 8:19,22). Our inward work

> receives the Son and is begotten as a son in the bosom of the heavenly Father . . . The outward work does not, but it receives its divine goodness by means of the inward work borne out and poured out in an emanation of the Deity.

In this same act of new creation, the Son is birthed and the Spirit flows out upon human history, and we are reborn as a lover like the Spirit of God. *It is the essence of the Son that I be born in him and in his image. It is the essence of the Holy Spirit that I should be burned into him and should be completely consumed in him and become entirely love.* In our work that is in God and therefore in Compassion and in Justice we *become entirely Love.* That is the goal of our work and of our being. But it is a goal without a goal, for love—like work—is *without a why.*

BOOKS BY MATTHEW FOX

Wrestling with the Prophets: Essays on Creation, Spirituality, and Everyday Life. San Francisco: Harper San Francisco, 1995.

The Reinvention of Work: A New Vision of Livelihood for Our Time. San Francisco: Harper San Francisco, 1994.

Sheer Joy: Conversations with Thomas Aquinas on Creation Spirituality, Foreword by Rupert Sheldrake, Afterword by Bede Griffith. San Francisco: Harper San Francisco, 1992.

Creation Spirituality: Liberating Gifts for the Peoples of the Earth. San Francisco: Harper San Francisco, 1992. Translated into Spanish, 1992.

Breakthrough: Meister Eckhart's Creation Spirituality in New Translation. Republished, New York: Image Books/Doubleday, 1991.

A Spirituality Named Compassion. Republished, San Francisco: Harper San Francisco, 1990.

The Coming of the Cosmic Christ: The Healing of Mother Earth and the Birth of a Global Renaissance. San Francisco: Harper San Francisco, 1988. *Vision Vom Kosmischen Christus,* translated into German, 1991.

Hildegard of Bingen's Book of Divine Works with Letters and Songs, edited by Matthew Fox. Santa Fe: Bear & Co., 1987.

Illuminations of Hildegard of Bingen, text by Hildegard of Bingen, commentary by Matthew Fox, Santa Fe: Bear & Co., 1985.

Original Blessing. Santa Fe: Bear & Co., 1983. Republished, London: Mountain Books, 1990. *Der Grosse Segen,* translated into German, 1991. *Adi Papamo Adimanugrahamo,* translated into Malayalam (Indian), 1992.

Manifesto for a Global Civilization, with physicist Brian Swimme. Santa Fe: Bear & Co., 1982.

Meditations with Meister Eckhart. Santa Fe: Bear & Co., 1982.

Western Spirituality: Historical Roots, Ecumenical Routes. Santa Fe: Bear & Co., 1981.

Whee! We, Wee All the Way Home: A Guide to Sensual, Prophetic Spirituality. Santa Fe: Bear & Co., 1976/1981.

On Becoming a Musical, Mystical Bear: Spirituality American Style. New York: Paulist Press, 1974.

Religion USA: Religion and Culture by Way of Time Magazine. Dubuque: Listening Press, 1971.